Just Keep Going

Just Keep Going

By Judy Davis

Published by Jebwizard Publishing

USA

ISBN-13: 978-1-7335264-4-9

Table of Contents

DEDICATION

Though many people helped get this journey started and finished, a few deserve special thanks.

To Nicole Dufresne and Mary Anne Stchur of the Boys & Girls Clubs of Providence, thank you for taking a chance on me and allowing me to do this on behalf of the Club.

To Beth and Mike Huber, thank you on so many levels. This wouldn't have happened without you.

To everyone who donated to the Boys & Girls Clubs on behalf of the ride. The kids will be swimming for decades to come because of your generosity.

Finally, to Jeanine McConaghy for helping me climb out of that dark hole all those years ago. Thank you.

FOREWORD

I first met Judy Davis in the fall of 2017 through Mary Anne Stchur, Chief Advancement Officer here at the Boys & Girls Clubs of Providence. She explained how Judy wanted to ride a bike across the country to raise funds for our swim programs. As the CEO, when approached with any new idea, the first question I ask is, "Why?" Mary Anne, already inspired and excited, told me about Judy's connection to our organization through our Master's Swim Program and her respect and adoration for our Aquatics Director, Ian Muir (a.k.a. The Swim Whisperer) Now intrigued myself, and knew I needed to meet her.

Once we met, I knew instantly we found another partner dedicated to creating a forever change in the lives of the city's most vulnerable children. From there the "Four Thousand Miles for Four Thousand Smiles" ride across the country was underway.

The project started with finding the right bike for Judy. After all, "Crazy Horse" would be Judy's only trusted friend consistently throughout her journey. Together, they battled hills, numerous corn fields, and WIND, pushed to their limits each day of their adventure.

Judy's philanthropic adventure began on June 29, 2018, in Eugene, Oregon, exactly the day she planned to leave. From there she pedaled through fifteen states, met hundreds of people and inspired people all over the country to think about their own dreams and goals.

She has proven you really can accomplish anything if you set your mind to it. Today, she is a true hero and local celebrity. I am also honored to call her my friend.

Judy's book is smart, witty, and heartwarming. When you read it, you feel as if you are right with her, meeting new people, learning about our wonderful country and possibly setting a goal of your own.

I am proud to report that to date Judy has raised $70,000 to create the' "Ian Muir Aquatics Endowment." Because of her, children and teens can learn to swim, not only now, but for generations to come. When she crossed the finish line on August 29, hundreds of boys and girls, family and friends and members of the community were at our Fox Point Clubhouse to welcome her and Crazy Horse home. She arrived on the exact day and time she had planned when mapping out her journey. On the hottest day of the year, she was all smiles and focused on chatting with our young members in awe of her accomplishment. She told them with great sincerity, it was all for them.

Judy is my Hometown Hero. I hope you enjoy reading about her adventures on the road. I have no doubt you will finish it knowing Judy's spirit and heart the way I do.

Enjoy the ride!

Nicole Dufresne,

CEO, Boys and Girls Clubs of Providence

TRANQUIL:

FREE FROM AGITATION OF MIND OR SPIRIT

PROLOGUE

Why do we do the things we do? It is an age-old question. I'm not talking about the little things. We go to the store because we need food or clothing, we go to school to get educated, we go inside when it rains to stay dry. The bigger question is why do we make certain major life choices? What type of career to pursue, where to live, who to associate with, what trips to take, what political party to associate with, what religion to follow, and so on?

When I told people I would spend a summer cycling across the United States, "Why?" was the number one question. The first few times it was almost shocking. The "why" hadn't crossed my mind. I knew it was the right thing to do. The second question was usually "where did you get the idea?" Finding myself at a moment I never expected, it just came to me, and I knew I had to do it. Why do people climb Mount Everest? Because it's there. Why swim the English Channel? Because it's there. Why run a marathon? To see if you can do it. Why sail around the world? To see if you can make it.

Many, many people told me they could never do something like this. My answer to them "it's not your thing" and "you don't have to." Everyone one of us challenges ourselves in different ways. Not everyone is cut out to climb Everest, swim the Channel, run a marathon, or cycle across the U.S. Hell, I didn't even know if I was cut out to ride across the U.S. You never know what may happen tomorrow to change the plan!

One thing that motivated me was to see the country from a different perspective. You can fly around to different places and visit or drive across the country and stop along the way. There's something about cycling that makes it somehow more real. Perhaps it's the pace, 50-100 miles a day mostly on side roads through small towns. You can whiz along an interstate at 80-90 miles an hour just to get to your next stop, but you will miss everything between. I believe it's the physical connection with your path, out in the elements, using your own power, that gives you a sense of where you are. You are part of the landscape, not just passing through. You see the details, engage with the people, not in passing but as part of their day, their life.

And they become part of yours.

I'm only halfway through this, and yet I've found many kindred spirits on their own "ride." The woman in Cambridge, Idaho who grew up on ranches, married a rancher, works with him on the ranch and opened bed and breakfast in town as her own project. The three partners in

Mitchell, Oregon—population 130—who opened a brewery in town because they love their beer and their town. The man in Jackson, Montana—population 32–who bought a dilapidated bunkhouse and turned it into the hub of the town. The woman veteran in Enderlin, North Dakota—population 900—who bought a local bar/restaurant with her husband, also a veteran, who keeps trying to make it better every day even though her husband succumbed to PTSD and committed suicide six months after they bought the place.

We do these things to see if we can.

I have always challenged myself mentally and physically, perhaps this ride is the culmination of those challenges. The proverbial icing on the cake. Perhaps, there will be something bigger. Who knows, though I'm sure it will come out of the blue like a lightning strike.

I've met many people along this journey and what has struck me the most is their reaction when I tell them what I'm doing. Most all think it's super cool and a great thing to do. When I'm in a small town and go to the local establishment I chat with residents, many have grown up in these towns and have worked their jobs for a while. As I tell my tale, they get a look of wonderment in their eyes. This has nothing to do with me but everything to do with them. They see the possibilities in their own lives; a new career, a move, their own journey. There is life beyond the mundane you just must be willing to act on it.

I suppose this is my plea to the world. When the idea strikes, grab it and reel it in. Don't think about why just think about how! It need not be a grand adventure; it could be as simple as rearranging the furniture in your house. Movement and action generate creativity and progress. They open doors and create new paths. Inactivity creates dust. Do not be embarrassed or intimidated when people question your motives, this is your journey, not theirs. We all walk our own path. How can someone on their path, with all its own obstacles, know what your path looks like. They can't so don't let them.

THE IDEA

Restless is the only way I can describe my mood in the early summer of 2017. Work was okay, friends were okay, everything was okay. Just that: okay. One night as I tossed and turned, willing sleep on myself, "it" came; the idea. I will cycle across the country! Forget sleep for the night, I was onto something big. At that moment, I wanted to get on my bike and start. The thoughts came rapid fire. How long would it take? How far would it be? What route should I choose? Can I pull it together for this summer?

I always wanted to see the country, not just see it, experience it. Often in my travels, I take backroads to wherever I am going. It's so much more interesting than interstates. It's not just getting from point A to point B, it's what's between those points. People, places, things. You miss all that going 75 miles an hour on the highway. Your destination is the only concern, and the faster you get there, the better. There is no thought about what might lie under the surface. It's all about completing whatever mission you are on. There's so much more to see and experience. Our country is a fabric woven together by each of our unique experiences.

Think about it, right from the get-go creative thought went into creating our country. The United States is "new" for a nation-state. We didn't evolve over thousands of years like the European countries and the Asian dynasties and countries. A group of individuals, from various parts of the then small colonies, planned the government United States. They took time to think about how we should govern ourselves, how we should exist. Each delegate to the Constitutional Convention brought their own life experiences and represented those of their constituencies. Done not be fiat, but by collaboration. There were flaws in those men and in the system they created, but I will leave that to the historians. The bottom line is we all have an inherent sense of the soul of our nation. It's represented by what people do with their lives. Most people understand that they can work to create their piece of the entire fabric.

I wanted to explore the country, talk to people, see what was happening in the vast "out there." Living in New England all my life was great, but I always felt we differed from the rest of the country. I wanted to discover what those differences and similarities were. This journey would not take me to all regions of the country, notably the south and southwest, but I figured I'd get a good picture through the Northwest, Midwest and Northeast states. You just can't do it in a car or by plane. You must be part of the environment, not just pass through it surrounded by metal and glass.

One night, discussing my plan with some dear friends, one of them suggested that I do the ride for a charity. "Hmm," I thought "that's a great idea." Besides once I committed publicly there would be no going back! The question became which charity. That was easy; the Boys & Girls Clubs of Providence, RI. It was a no-brainer as I had been swimming in a Master's program at their Fox Point club for several years. I got to know the staff, particularly the Aquatics Director, Ian Muir.

Ian is a true inspiration, one of the most unassuming people I have ever met. A consummate coach, he's in his early 70's, and swimming is his passion. Ian took over the program at the club twenty years ago. When the pool was a disgrace, and I'm sure the club was considering closing it down to save the expense. Ian came along and transformed it and the swim program into a true gem. My fellow Masters who swim at other locations always say Fox Point is the best-maintained pool they swim at. His true passion is teaching kids how to swim and how to compete. Occasionally, one of his prodigies will join us for a master's session while they're home on break from college. He is so proud of them and their accomplishments. He simply beams. Thousands of Providence kids have been through his program with great success. I often think of how many lives he's saved because the kids know how to swim.

I've had more than a few coaches throughout my athletic life and would rank Ian right up at the top. He knows how to push your buttons and get you to go beyond your self-inflicted limits. He considers everything from technique to speed and motivates. Coaching can be a delicate thing between mentor and mentee, in my experience, the best coaches speak to you in a way you "get." Sometimes it's a simple explanation of the technique that just clicks in your mind, and you understand what to do.

Given all that, it was easy to pick the Club. Pools are expensive to maintain, why not create an endowment for their aquatics programs to ensure their continued viability.

I've read many books and listened to a lot of podcasts about success and achievement. One theme often involved is that by doing for others your efforts will come back around to you and open doors and avenues to success that may not have existed before. Taking on a cause changed the world for me. Suddenly there was a greater purpose. Sure, I still had my own reasons for taking this on, my personal life journey, but doing it to make other people's lives better was the icing on the cake. I've met and experienced so many new people and things, liberating.

When our swim program started in the Fall of 2017, I couldn't wait to tell the people at the Boys and Girls Club about my idea. The first day back I hunted down Ryan, the Director of the Fox Point Club, and excitedly told him what I wanted to do.

"Ryan, I'm riding my bike across the country next summer, and I'm doing it to raise money for the club's swim programs." It took a minute to sink in with him, I could see his mind working through it.

"Wow, really? You're going to pedal a bike across the country?"

"Yes sir, I am. Can you set up a meeting with the development people?"

"I certainly will," he replied.

Now locked into this adventure, not that for one moment from the time I conceived it until I finished did I doubt I would do it, but now I stood committed. A few weeks later, Ryan and I met with Mary Anne, the development director, and Nicole, the CEO of the Providence Clubs. Mary Anne was new to the Rhode Island area but had a career in development for non-profits. She was excited to hear about my plan and explained that in her last job at the DuPont Hospitals in Delaware she had run a similar campaign. One of the hospital's corporate counsel rode from Florida to Pennsylvania to raise money for the children's wing of the hospital. She said he had raised over $100,000 for the cause. That was amazing. I had been thinking much smaller than that, maybe $20-$25 thousand. As usual, I was underestimating myself!

We agreed it would be a great project. I told them I would work on a mission statement and think about potential corporate donors. One thing my circuitous journey through life has created is a large and diverse network of friends, many of whom own businesses and are influential in the community.

I went home and started on my homework! Writing the mission statement "You Gotta Have a Goal" brought the whole project into focus. I had always been more energized and alive when I was working toward something. In reviewing the course of the last fifty plus years, it was clear I was more fulfilled and focused when I had a project. The list is long, law school, running a marathon, passing the Bar exam, reading the hundred greatest novels of the 20th century, playing competitive golf, starting my law firm. The goals get bigger, and satisfaction greater. I wanted the kids at the club to understand they could achieve great things if they put their mind to it. If they had an idea to seize it and take a chance. There is a big world beyond Providence, Rhode Island and they could go anywhere and do anything. Nothing should stop them.

PLANNING

I t was game on for my adventure, now came the planning. I focused on the mission. It was ten months away, but sometimes felt like it was happening tomorrow or that the day would never get here. There is something to the concept of focusing on the big idea, and the details will fall into place along the way.

The first big decision was, "when." I knew it had to be summer because work slows down. The great thing about Rhode Island is it's a tremendous summer place. The season is short but intense. Everyone seems to enjoy the outdoors, beaching, boating, cycling, golf. I won't say work comes to a complete stop, but it slows down. People kept asking me how are you going to take two months away from work. The answer - preparation. I devote much of my law practice to criminal defense, so I'm in court most days. The courts excuse lawyers from appearing when you go on vacation or are working on something that demands focus. The presiding justices of the courts must approve your request. Since I was away for two months, I also had to name a backup attorney if something came up with any of my clients.

Somehow, I had a sense this would take me two months. I'm not sure how I came up with that, but it sounded reasonable, so I filed my court excuses for the dates of June 28, 2018, through August 31, 2018. This gave me until Labor Day to do it. I got the court excuse in early, as the ride drew closer, I could schedule things around those months without push-back from judges. I prepped my clients I would not be around all summer so when the time came to take off my mind was at ease that the decks were clear until Labor Day. Besides, I wouldn't be on Mars. I'd have access to my cell phone and email if something important came up.

Once I set the dates, I had to put this adventure together. I needed a bike, equipment, and a route. When this idea struck me in the spring of 2017, I wanted to get on the bike and just go, right then, that summer. I suppose I could have pulled it off, though it would have been haphazard and likely led to many more problems. I never could have achieved the charitable piece that quickly. We needed time to get the word out and get corporate and individual sponsorship. That kind of thing takes time and planning as I soon discovered.

THE BIKE

The bike would be the most critical piece of equipment on the journey. I had zero experience with bicycle touring. It became funny both before and during the ride, people would ask me about my experience with this type of thing. I must have been doing this for years, you know smaller trips, a week here and there, maybe weekends. Nope, I had done none of that. I had only been riding for a few years, and it was road cycling, very different from touring. When you see people out on their road bikes they're probably out for a morning or afternoon, 10, 25, 50, maybe 100 miles. All they need is water and a spare tube in case of a flat. In a few hours, they're done. When bicycle touring, you're out for multiple days or weeks, so you need a lot more gear. Camping gear, clothes, bike gear, extra tubes, a tire, a chain, and tools are all necessary. You can't just hop on the bike and go.

I knew my road bike was not up to the task, they just can't handle the weight of the gear and the variety of terrain. I researched touring bikes and found that not all the bike companies made them and if they did there might be one or two models. It came down to two companies, Trek and Surly. The Trek 520 is one of the first real "touring" bikes produced beginning in the 1970s. It remains largely unchanged. They now have models with a few more bells and whistles based on the 520. The Surly Disc Trucker was also pointed out as a great touring bike. With that in mind, I had to find the actual bike that would accompany me on this odyssey.

In our planning meetings, Nicole and Mary Anne told me not to buy anything as they would see if there were any sponsorship opportunities with my gear. Perhaps we could get a bike donated or at least a reduced price. They contacted two local shops, one that carried Surly and one that carried Trek. One thing you have to know about bike shops is they are owned and run by cyclists. It's an almost cultish world where they speak a language a non-cyclist would never understand. Every time I go into a shop, I learn a new term of art, it's funny. Cyclists are into riding and gear, not so much the business end of the deal. They can tell you what year a particular model came out and take it apart with their eyes closed. Ask them how their first-quarter sales went or how they plan to advertise for the coming year, and you may get a shoulder shrug. In my limited experience, the best shops are small, almost hole in the wall places where cycling groupies gather to speak in their tongues. Don't get me wrong, these guys and gals are phenomenal people who will do whatever they can to help you get back on the road as fast as they can, just don't ask about "business stuff."

Of the two shops, only one responded. I imagine the shops are inundated with people like me walking in off the street and say "Hey, I'm doing a super long cycle tour to raise money for {insert charity here}. Can you give me a bike?" Thus, it's understandable they are skeptical about these requests. That's why I suggested the Club contact the shops, after all, they are part of a high-profile national organization. I wanted the shops to know this was a serious fundraising event – not just some crazy lark. The shop that responded, NBX Bikes, has several locations in Rhode Island and does more marketing so a little more up on the business piece.

We reached out in late January which should have given us plenty of time to have the bike squared away for a late June departure date. I was excited. This is the most essential piece of equipment I would need for this journey.

After phone calls and emails over a few weeks, the Club got a response. The shop's marketing guy would "check into it." Sounded promising but several more weeks of silence ensued. I started to worry. It was such an unknown. Would the bike have to be ordered? Would it be in stock? Would my size be available? Finally, I got involved in the email chain and suggested that we'd be getting the bike from them, discount or not, and I'd be going over to the East Providence store to check out models and sizes, etc. He said "Fine, I'll let them know you're coming."

I went to the store that weekend and talked to some sales people I know and explained they should have heard from the marketing guy. The message hadn't trickled down.

It's now March, and I'm getting antsy, I wanted to get used to whatever bike I'd get before I started a 4,000-mile tour! We talked about Trek's touring bikes and checked them out online. They don't stock them because there's not a huge demand, but they can order you one. Then one guy suggested a brand-new Trek model, the Checkpoint. It's a "gravel bike." A hybrid between a pure mountain bike and a road bike. It can handle touring and has plenty of options to attach racks, etc. That it weighs about six pounds less than the 520, is also a big deal. I was hooked, I had to have the Checkpoint. The only problem was the model I liked was about $700.00 more than the 520 and didn't come with any racks like the 520 did. They also had my size in stock, a lovely British Racing Green-- seriously – it was meant to be!

The communication from the marketing people was still sporadic, but I clung to hope. At least I knew I could get the bike I wanted even if they wouldn't give me a break on the price. This was a relief.

A few days after visiting the shop and getting hooked on the Checkpoint, I was at City Hall in East Providence recording documents for a client. As I walked out of the building, a large SUV pulled up to the curb in front of the building emblazoned with the bike shop's logo all over it. You might be thinking "what a coincidence" however, Rhode Islander's will tell you it's not unusual. We are a tiny state, and a five-minute conversation between total strangers generally leads to them discovering that they know at least one person in common, probably more like five. Heck, they may even be related! If there are six degrees of separation in the rest of the world, there are two degrees in Rhode Island.

The driver got out as I exited the building. "You're not Don by chance?" I asked him.

"No, I'm Matt." He replied.

"Okay, I've been working on something with Don."

"Well, what's up? I'm the owner." I laughed. This was too good to be true. Here we were having difficulty communicating with these folks, and the owner just pops up on the street in front of me. A true Rhode Island moment.

"I'm doing a cross-country ride to benefit the Boys & Girls Clubs of Providence, and I'm looking for a bike."

"That's YOU?" he exclaimed. "We were just talking about you the other day! That's great, what a good cause." We chatted for a few minutes about the East Providence shop and about the Checkpoint. He agreed it was an awesome bike. We parted ways, and he said I'd be hearing from Don.

Being the impatient sort, I am, a couple of days later, I emailed Don and told him about meeting Matt and wanting to get the Checkpoint. He responded quickly. "Well, Trek was willing to give you a 520. I'll have to talk to them about the Checkpoint." OMG! They were going to

13

GIVE me a bike! I couldn't believe it. I figured they might give me a discount, but I wasn't betting on it. He came back a few days later and said Trek wouldn't outright give me the Checkpoint, but I would have to pay only the cost difference between the two. Beautiful! I was getting a pricey bike for $700.00! Grateful doesn't even come close. I didn't want this trip to break the bank as I wouldn't have a paycheck for two months, this would be a big help.

I was at the shop the next day picking up the bike! Thankfully, Don had alerted at least one person, Pete, the store manager. Pete was great. Now that the bike was in place it would need racks, panniers, and lights, etc. He was the man for the job. "Don't worry about anything. I'll get you everything you need." Perfect, it was getting on toward May, and I had to wrap up a few projects for work before taking the rest of the summer off. I also needed to get in cycling shape! I didn't have time to research everything I would need, price it and order it.

THE ROUTE

I t's a big country, and I had to figure out the best way to get across it. It had to be a northern route, the prospect of riding through Texas and Arizona in high heat wasn't an option. I also had to decide whether it would be east to west or west to east. My initial inclination was east to west. I had contacts stretching across New York State and Ohio so as I was settling into the ride I would be with some familiar faces. However, the more I thought about it, it became increasingly clear that west to east was the way to go. Every day I would get a little closer to home, a big incentive. In theory, the prevailing wind is from the west so that should be helpful too.

I turned to the computer to search for the best routes for cycling across the country. Many sites came up, but I discovered the Adventuring Cycling Association based in Missoula, Montana had an extensive route network with over 47,000 miles of routes across the United States. Their web site and maps became invaluable during the ride. I cobbled together several of their routes to see the places I wanted to see. Their most famous is the Transamerica Trail starting in Astoria, Oregon and finishing in Yorktown, Virginia. An annual self-supported race covering the course. In 2018, the winner did it in 17 days, 8 hours and 58 minutes. Wrap your head around that for a minute! 3,200 miles in 17 days!

I wanted to go through states I had never been to, the Northwest and upper Midwest. I decided to start in Florence, Oregon, an off-shoot of the Transamerica which begins in Astoria. It would have been great to start in Astoria, but it would have added over 250 miles to a journey of close to 4,000 miles. I just didn't have the time. For the first couple of legs, I'd be on the Transamerica through Oregon and then move on to the Lewis and Clark Trail into Idaho and Montana. Being a history buff tracing Lewis and Clark's footsteps was right up my alley. I would stay on the Lewis & Clark until Dickinson, North Dakota then pick up the Northern Tier route. It would take me across the rest of North Dakota into Minnesota down the Mississippi through Wisconsin and Iowa then across into Illinois on to Indiana and Ohio finally up the coast of Lake Erie to Buffalo. From Buffalo in I would wing it. I have spent a lot of time in Western and Central NY State having gone to Hobart & William Smith Colleges in Geneva and still have a lot of friends there. The final stretch would be down through Massachusetts and Connecticut into Rhode Island and home. Nothing to it right1 It mapped out right around 4,000 miles.

Once I had nailed down the route, I ordered all the hard copy maps from Adventure Cycling. Many people questioned having hard copies, but it was the way to go. I had no idea what cell service would be like, and there was always the possibility of running out of battery life on the phone. Their maps are also great because they give you much more than just the route information. They outline the riding conditions of each segment, elevations and surface types. I came to rely heavily on them, especially elevations! They also listed services such as places to stay and eat, post offices and, most crucial, bike shops. They made my life much more relaxed; I could rest assured I knew where I was going.

TRAINING

How does one train for a two-month, four-thousand-mile bike tour? Honestly, I'm not sure you can, in any traditional sense. I'm speaking as someone generally fit who works out several times a week. If you've been sitting on the couch for the last twenty years munching on potato chips and ice cream, you would need to get to a level of fitness to even consider doing this. Even if you are an athlete or a cyclist, there's no way to train as you would for, say, a marathon. For that, you'd start a weekly schedule several months before the race and gradually increase your long runs up to twenty miles, then back off the miles a week or two before the race. The key concept is that it is "a" race which takes place on a single day, not a two-month journey riding stretches of four to six days in a row.

Most people work, so riding 500-600 miles a week to train is impractical. I did little training on the bike before I started, choosing my usual swim workouts three days a week from September to mid-June and a run or ride once or twice a week. I'm not a winter rider and don't enjoy battling cold and snow, so I didn't ride until late April, only two months before the departure date. I'd go for longer 50-mile rides on the weekends and tried to build up to longer rides on back to back days to prepare for multiple days in the saddle. During the week I'd try to get out for shorter rides, but that gets difficult with work.

I didn't get my bike until about a month before I left and the rest of the gear was coming in piecemeal, so I had little opportunity to ride fully loaded. There was a problem getting my front rack, so I didn't ride with front panniers until I hit the road in Oregon! Trial by fire if ever there was one.

There's a huge difference between riding a road bike and a fully loaded touring bike, so some of the training I did that spring wasn't realistic. I didn't have a choice as my bike wasn't ready, but just being in a saddle had to be helpful. The bike loaded was between 70 and 80 lbs., well over half my body weight so riding around on my 22-pound road bike wouldn't help much.

The other training issue was terrain. Rhode Island and southeastern Massachusetts, where I do most of my riding, are mostly flat. How could I possibly train to climb the Cascades and the Rockies when the highest point in the entire state of Rhode Island is 965 feet?? I suppose I could have headed up to New Hampshire or Vermont to get some hill work in but the weeks leading to my departure were slipping away. Plus, I had so many other things to take care of before leaving for the summer. I would just have to hope I could handle the 4'300' climb up McKenzie Pass to 5,325' on the third day of my tour. Yikes!

Mental preparation was perhaps more important than physical. As I've mentioned, in the year leading to my departure the ride was always foremost in my mind. Not a day went by when I didn't spend an inordinate amount of time just thinking about how I would do this. Having the annotated maps was a huge help. I could read up on the terrain I would face and the general conditions of the roads. I spent so much time going over those maps, especially the beginning legs, that when I got there, it felt as if I'd been before. Well not exactly there, but you get what I mean.

As a life-long athlete, I knew I could push my body to the outer limit as I had done through soccer and lacrosse games in college and many half marathons and a marathon. I knew I could withstand pain. I have only run one marathon, but it is an example. The first 20 miles flew by in 2:50 then suddenly my legs cramped uncontrollably. My mind and my lungs were great, I yelled at my legs to keep going. I had to limp through the last 6.2 miles trying to stretch out cramping calves and quads along the way. It took an hour to cover those last miles, and it was painful, but there was no way I would not finish.

It's experiences like those that gave me the confidence I would complete this journey. I knew it would be trying and challenging, but I never doubted I could do it mentally. Though having absolutely no experience with bike touring made it difficult to imagine precisely "how" I would do it. It would be like playing in a golf tournament at a course you've never played, not even a practice round. You don't know what to expect or know where the hazards are, but you get up there and swing away. Often those are excellent rounds because you have no expectations. I could only hope that the ride would be the same!

For perspective on some of my training here are a couple of pre-trip blog posts.

From Jude's Jargon:

Perseverance Road

May 28, 2018

Went for a training ride today, getting ready for my big cross-country adventure. Headed down to Tiverton to do the Little Compton - Westport fifty-mile loop. The day dawned overcast and cool. I slept a little later than usual, but hey, it's a holiday Monday so why not?? It would be a test. I'd ridden forty miles Saturday, twenty-five yesterday and shooting for fifty today. It's a far cry from the eighty per day I hope to average starting a month from now, but you must start somewhere.

The loop is one of the most scenic in the RI/MA area. It meanders along the Sakonnet River toward the Point in Little Compton. Water on one side farms and marshes on the other. Suddenly the water is gone, and you're in farmland, the cows gazing solemnly at you as you pass. It's the land that time forgot as you go through the Commons, which probably hasn't changed too much in the last hundred years or so. There's a church, post office, diner, and small grocery - who needs more than that? You get to wind your way through the woods for a while and then the ocean appears again as you go through Acoaxcet by Elephant Rock Beach, the stately summer homes quiet on the edge of summer. Eventually, you make your way through Westport by the town beach and then Horseneck State Beach. Having done the loop a couple of times previously, I knew I had about 12-13 miles to go. I felt good; my legs were a little sore but not overly so. I knew there were two fairly big hills to deal with, I began to mentally prepare.

The first comes when you turn off Route 88 and head back toward Little Compton. It's short but steep. I take it on and push through, out of breath with screaming quads at the top. Catch your breath, take a drink and keep your legs moving! The route gently rolls along for the next few miles, equally up and down so plenty of time to coast. I make the next turn onto a winding country road which I recalled being a fun stretch. I glanced up and spotted a battered old wooden road sign "Perseverance Rd." It was sublimely perfect at that moment in time.

I thought about "perseverance" as I glided by the farmhouses along the way. Not sure whether I was in Rhode Island or Massachusetts, though it hardly mattered as the American flags waving from the porches said it all on this Memorial Day. My first thought was the long hill coming up at the 45-mile mark. The first time I did the loop, it ate me up and spit me out. Today I was ready to persevere and spit it right back! Slowly my focus changed as I passed more flags and a few small historic cemeteries, where many graves had brand new flags to commemorate the Veterans buried there.

Yes, my hill would be tough, though compared to Bunker Hill, Gettysburg, the Meuse-Argonne, Normandy or Iwo Jima it was nothing. Those young soldiers who kept moving forward with chaos all around, their friends bleeding and dying at their feet. They had to keep going, keep pedaling, don't stop. I would conquer my hill today, safe with the knowledge that but for the perseverance of those brave souls I wouldn't be free to conquer all the hills that lay ahead. Peace.

From Jude's Jargon:

Meaningful Miles

June 10, 2018

Four summers ago, I was out for a run, my usual four miles on the Turner Reservoir bike path when I realized that my whole body hurt. I had been a runner for the better part of thirty-five years, and now my body was screaming at me - ENOUGH! People would ask "Is it your knees? Hips?" The answer was no - it was everything. My body just ached. The next day I went out and bought a bike.

Through the years I'd known several people who biked who told me I'd love it. I always argued it was too time consuming, I would have to ride for an hour and a half to get the same workout as a five-mile run. Well, that is true; however, my body didn't hurt anymore! I could get out of bed in the morning without being stiff and sore! It started as just a workout, maybe do fifteen miles at lunchtime with a few friends, perhaps twenty-five or thirty on the weekend. Then it became kind of like running, just get the workout in and be done with it. As some of my riding friends will tell you, I just don't like to stop. "Come on! Can't we just keep going and move on to whatever's next for the day."

Last summer after I decided to do the cross-country ride, I started to up my mileage, fifty to sixty miles in a day. I was riding a road bike and really didn't stop. I had plenty of water with me and could eat a granola bar as I rode so why bother stopping? This spring started much the same, just get the miles in to get ready for the trip. Then, last week, it all changed.

NBX bike shop got my bike fitted out with racks and panniers so I could train loaded. What a difference twenty-five pounds makes! It will probably be closer to forty when I start the trip. Last weekend I did forty miles Saturday and fifty-seven Sunday on relatively flat terrain. It was different but not bad. It was a good start, but I knew that I would have to ramp it up some to get used to doing even more mileage daily.

This week I did twenty-five on Thursday and Friday morning before work, then a fifty-seven loop on Saturday. These rides are flat, a few hills but nothing like what I will see early in my trip when I head through the Cascades and the northern Rockies. I'm truly a little nervous about this. My third day out I will go over McKenzie Pass in Oregon, just a little 4,000- foot climb! So today I changed it up a little and threw fifty miles into the Route Genius app in MapMyRide. It gave me a course which headed west through Rhode Island. Winding through Pawtucket, Providence, Johnston, Scituate, Coventry, West Warwick, Warwick, Cranston, Providence and home to Rumford. I swear Johnston is just one big hill with Scituate at the bottom of it! So, I got in plenty of hills today.

What started as a nice fifty-mile ride became a seventy-mile odyssey! A few missed turns leading to more hills, losing my battery at 53 miles thus having to improvise the route to get to places I knew. Before I knew it, I was six hours into a four-hour ride. Nevertheless, it was a great day. Saw some fabulous Rhode Island sites along the way starting with Slater Mill, the birthplace of the Industrial Revolution, and winding up through Pawtuxet Village where the neighborhood was celebrating the "real" start of the American Revolution by burning a replica of the British customs schooner the HMS Gaspee. Sorry, all you Massachusetts peeps, the war started in Rhode Island when John Brown and his boys decided over a few pints one night to row down the bay from Providence and burn the schooner which had run aground on a sandbar while chasing one of their merchant ships. The first blood of the war was shed that night during the conflict.

All in all, a good day. I feel a bit more prepared. Ready for McKenzie Pass!

SOLO JOURNEY

When I shared the idea with a few close friends, they were generally supportive, though I could sense their apprehension. "You're going to do this by yourself?"

"Of course, I am."

These friends knew me well enough to know I meant it and frankly wouldn't do it any other way. I should tell you I am, by character, somewhat of a loner. Not that I don't have many fabulous relationships, because I do. I am lucky to count many, many people from all over as close friends. It's just to say I spend an inordinate amount of time alone. I have lived alone for over 30 years. I have my own solo legal practice, my dog as my assistant. It's rather embarrassing when she snores during client meetings. I am comfortable being on my own.

The thought of doing this with someone never entered my mind. When you're with a friend or a group, you keep to yourselves. I wanted to be forced to meet people and share life with them. How else was I going to discover what's going on in this big ole country? The other issue is the actual travel. When you are with a group, you are at the mercy of the group. If someone doesn't feel well and doesn't want to ride that day you're stuck. I wanted to go at my pace and see what I wanted to see, talk to who I wanted to talk to. That just wouldn't be possible with more than just me.

It's often said that each phase of your life serves a specific purpose. That your experiences, added together, lead you to where you're meant to be. Planning this journey caused me to believe it is entirely correct. I've done many things in my life, often with seemingly no purpose. I never felt I knew why I was doing any one thing I took on. Always searching for what I wanted to be in life. I wandered through diverse careers; ski shop manager, police officer, lawyer, coach, business development, back to lawyer without ever feeling it was right. When I started working on the idea of the ride, it all fell into place.

I found I was older than most I met on the road. Many were kids in their 20's just starting out in life experience. While I'm sure they were having a blast taking their journey, I'm so happy to have done it later in life so my many experiences would shape my perception. For instance, working as a police officer, you learn more about people and their circumstances than you can anywhere else. It's basic humanity. You see people at their best and their worst. Think about it, no one calls the cops because they're having a good day. You learn to understand that everyone is different and can't be treated the same way. You learn to judge character and read people. Working as a prosecutor and as a criminal defense attorney also contributed significantly to those things. You manage expectations and learn to communicate on every level. There are times for compassion and times for hard-nosed reality. As a coach and athlete, I've had to motivate myself and players to go beyond comfort zones. It is only there you discover what you're capable of, your limits.

I wanted this to be my journey, selfishly. I wanted no one else's life experience to cloud what was happening. To view everything and everyone one through my own lens, the lens created by my personal experiences leading to that specific moment.

The further I was from beginning the journey people would kind of brush past the fact that I was going alone. It was months away, and they seemed to doubt it would ever happen, never mind I would do it alone. I'm sure that was the sentiment of the people at the Boys & Girls Club. They didn't know me from a hole in the wall, and yet here I was taking on a serious endeavor in their name. My friends knew I could do this., They knew me, knew what I was made of, and had seen me take on other significant challenges. Nicole and Mary Anne had no such knowledge. For all they knew I was a total crackpot who would make it a hundred miles and give up because it was too hard.

Watching people react to the solo nature of the trip was the best. Folks would inquire about my plan, and I explained it would be my first touring trip, almost 4,000 miles across the country by myself. More than a few jaws hit the floor. "Seriously??? You've never done this before, and you're going across the country alone!!!" "Yup – hey, go big or go home!" Besides if stuff is going to go wrong it can go wrong on a weekend trip or a two-month journey. There's no way to know what's going to happen, so you just do it.

It was entertaining to explain the trip to my "AG Girlfriends." We are a group of seven female lawyers who became good friends while working as prosecutors at RI Department of Attorney General in the late '90s. In Rhode Island, because the state is so small, there are no District Attorney's offices and the Attorney General handles all criminal prosecutions. All seven of us worked in various sections of the Criminal Division, prosecuting everything from D.U.I.'s and simple assaults to rape and murder. It would be an understatement to say there are no shrinking violets among us. We've seen crime up close and personal while trying to lead normal lives with families and everything that goes with that. We've embarrassed more than a few young waiters when they approach our table to discover that the conversation is about graphic crime scenes and situations.

We had gathered for dinner one night in the early spring of 2018. For once we were all there, a difficult feat considering the jobs and family responsibilities everyone has. Everyone was chatting around the table in small groups, and I was sitting next to my friend Jeanine telling her about the trip. We talked about the details, and it came out that I was going solo.

"Wait just a minute!" she exclaimed. "You're doing this by yourself?"

"Of course, I am," I replied.

She called out to everyone at the table, "you have to hear what Judy's doing this summer."

I told them the plan to ride cross-country. Jeanine then added the bombshell, "and she's going by herself." The discussion of how cool the concept of the ride vanished, and the tone degenerated into chaos.

"No, you're NOT!" my friend Kathy exclaimed.

"No, no, no!" said Bethany.

Remember we are all still working in the world of criminal law, there's a boogeyman around every corner waiting to rape and murder some poor unsuspecting cyclist like me!

"How are we going to know where you are? You need a GPS chip, so we'll be able to find you when you're kidnapped!" Stacey, the Chief of the AG's Criminal Division said, "I'll alert the state police in every state you're going through!"

Once everyone calmed down, we discussed it more, and I assured them they would know where I was, and everything would be fine. I told them, despite what they might think, most people were helpful and friendly.

While still skeptical, they agreed it would be a great adventure for a great cause. Besides, I would be in the United States, not Afghanistan! They do have electricity and cell phone service outside of New England!

The skepticism from my colleagues in the criminal justice system didn't stop there. Shortly after the dinner, I was in a chamber's conference discussing a murder case I would be defending with co-counsel, an AG, and the judge. We were trying to determine when to schedule the trial. My co-counsel was coming off several very intense trials and was looking for a break before this one began while the judge wanted to do it soon.

The judge is something of a workaholic and handles the "gun calendar" in Providence County. He's most always got a trial going with another waiting on deck. Defendants who come before him are justifiably nervous as he's known for handing down tough sentences. Because many of the gun laws call for mandatory consecutive sentences--most convicted defendants won't see freedom for many years-- decades in most cases. He looks the part as well, standing over 6'5" with a shock of white hair and a deep voice. When he pronounces a sentence from the bench, it's like a God on judgment day.

I explained I would be unavailable in July and August as I would be out of state. I was sitting directly across the desk from the judge and told him I'd be cycling cross-country.

"Tell me you're not doing that by yourself?" he said staring at me intently.

"I am," I declared.

He took a deep sigh and said, "Judy, I'm very concerned about you doing this by yourself. Are you going to be carrying anything with you?"

He meant a gun as he knew I was a former police officer. I hadn't made a final decision on the issue but was leaning against it. Frankly, guns are heavy, and it would be a lot to worry about. My philosophy has also been when you bring a gun somebody gets shot, so don't bring a gun. His concern was touching.

COUNTDOWN

When the idea for the ride first came up I wanted to take it on immediately. I would lie in bed at night, especially that first night, and try to think of a way to get going as soon as possible. How hard could it be? Just get a bunch of gear together, get on the bike and head west. My rational brain took over, and I realized this would take planning. Perhaps had I been twenty-one instead of 51 I would have just jumped on the bike and taken off. After looking at it rationally, July and August of 2018 would be the time to do it. It was still over a year away, a seemingly infinite amount of time.

I spent the summer of 2017 talking about it with close friends. It didn't feel real, just the light at the end of a long tunnel. I would take time and research things like routes and bikes, but it was random, a Google search here or there. I was focused on the trip; it was front of mind from the moment I had the idea. However, with all that time ahead of me before it happened, there was no sense of urgency to plan. Every month I would stress out, feeling like I should be doing something constructive. That would make me do more research which calmed me down for the time being.

After the first of the year, the clock ticked faster. I was getting more stressed about everything, especially the fundraising piece. It was frustrating, I felt like we had to get the word out in some organized fashion. How would we raise tens of thousands of dollars if we waited too long? Having never run a fundraising campaign, I had no idea what to expect. Mary Anne and Nicole didn't seem worried, but I sure was. Fundraising is their lives. Their very existence as an organization depends almost solely on fundraising. They knew what they were doing, knew the steps and time line. It became funny. I was beyond stressed about raising the money, and they were stressing about me doing the ride. Had we only stayed in our own lanes there would have been no stress – they had no doubt they could raise the money, and I had no doubt I could do the ride.

Looking back on it, I can see why they were so worried about the ride piece. I just walked in off the street and told them about my plan. They didn't know me, let alone well enough to know I could accomplish this. They didn't know my past, my determination, my athletic history to know when I said I could do it I meant it. I could have been some crazy yahoo full of ideas that never happened. Though we haven't discussed it, I'm sure there were internal conversations at the Club about who the heck I was and if I could be serious about this endeavor. Maybe the rationale was to hold off on the publicity until we have a better idea of who this person is and what she's capable of. I suspect it was as stressful for them as it was for me in the weeks and months leading to my departure.

The stress added up as we got into the spring months. Getting the bike was taking longer than anticipated. I didn't have everything in place until a few days before leaving. I remember heading over to the bike shop on my way back from the courthouse about two weeks before leaving. We were still waiting on my front racks. The ones initially ordered weren't right. I was stressing. Pete picked up on it right away. "You seem a little wound up." He said. "Well, I have a lot of stuff to do for work in the next two weeks, and all my gear isn't here, so yes, I'm wound up," I replied. He laughed. "We'll get you ready." I trusted him, but I was nervous that I wouldn't pull it all together.

The other problem was that other than Nicole and Mary Anne, no one had any idea of the pressure. I had spent so much time thinking about this, and now it would happen. I would tell people what I was planning. They would show interest, "oh really, that's cool" or "wow, what an adventure." It was just conversational, they didn't seem to grasp the entire concept, almost as if I were talking about driving out to the Cape for the weekend. "Oh, that's nice, it will be lovely this time of year." Didn't they get it??? I would be on my bike alone for two months! It was scary! Part of it was that I hadn't done it yet. It was such a huge undertaking people could not conceptualize it until I started. Besides everyone had their own stuff going on, work, family, friends, no need to take on my stress.

As it got down to the final week before departure, it got more real. My siblings and close friends felt my angst. To everyone's relief, I found a good GPS app for my phone. I could share my location with selected people, so they knew where I was. This was a blessing and a curse as there would be a few occasions I lost cell coverage. I was suddenly totally "off the grid." More stressful for them than for me. Hey, I knew where I was, and I was okay!

There were details to attend to, after all who would take care of "my children," the pets? We held a "pet meeting" so everyone was on the same page for the food and walking routines. The cat would be easy. She could stay at home, and my sister would check in every day or so. The dog was more complicated. She's a rescue and had been severely abused in the three years before I got her. Change is hard for her, she's often anxious. She would split time between my friends, Beth and Mike, and my sister, Nancy. Knowing them all, she'd be comfortable, but it would be different without me for two months. How she would react was a mystery. We were all a little anxious.

I was nervous, thinking I may embark on this journey and see none of them again. Though none expressed it, I'm sure the thought crossed their minds. It's not unheard of for cyclists to get hit by cars or trucks or to run into that mysterious serial killer in some random town.

More than once I wondered as I heard trucks coming up behind me on a narrow, two lane road, "is this it? Am I going to get taken out right now?" Unnerving.

Separation Anxiety

June 23, 2018

I quickly got into my car and pulled out of the lot. I simply couldn't look back for fear of breaking down. "Would she be okay?" "Did I pack everything she'd need?" "Would they take care of her and make sure she didn't get hurt on the long trip?" "Would she miss me?" "Could I survive without her?"

You might think I was sending my first-born off to college or even my beloved dog off for a summer adventure. But, alas, I was merely shipping my bike out to Oregon! In the short 2 months I've had her we've become close. We'd already spent 600 or 700 hundred miles together in preparation for the 4,000-mile odyssey! I'd grown used to the weight of the racks and panniers, the sound of the wheels spinning as I coasted down hills. It's a very comfortable ride and feels like we're a unit as

38

we roll around Rhode Island and southeastern Massachusetts.

I dropped her off at the shop so they could pack her up with much of my gear and ship her the following day. We were trying to get as much in the box as possible, and I knew they'd have to take her apart to fit everything. The thought of watching that happen was scary. I just wanted to walk into the shop in Oregon and have her waiting for me. I sighed with relief when Pete at the shop texted to say that all was well and she was ready to go, though he made reference to a Rubik's cube that made me cringe.

The bike and I are a team. If she doesn't perform, I won't make it and if I don't neither will she! With that in mind, I felt she needed a name. We'd have a lot of time to talk, so I should at least call her something. I put it out to my friends, and one said, "something presidential or at least historical." (As an aside I name my pets after presidents or other historical figures: the cat is Teddy Roosevelt, the dog is Margaret Thatcher.) The suggestion made sense. Another friend said how about "Comanche" the famous war-horse. Hmm an Indian theme - she was onto something! I was reading Ron Chernow's biography of Ulysses Grant and was at the point in his presidency when he was dealing with Indian issues in the western

39

states. Notably mentioned were Sitting Bull and Crazy Horse both great Indian warriors. All the references were to places in southern Montana, which coincidentally is my route!

Crazy Horse, a Sioux warrior, sounded like a strong possibility so I did a little research and discovered that his given Indian name was "Cha-O-Ha" which translates to "in the wilderness" or "among the trees." Bingo! This journey is all about being in the wilderness! So Crazy Horse or Cha-O-Ha it is! Though these friends think the "crazy" part more apropos! Can't say I disagree!

Crazy Horse and I will be reunited this Thursday when I arrive in Florence, Oregon. I hope she'll be in one piece and ready to go. I hope I will be too. Can't wait to start the adventure!

AND WE'RE OFF

I t was time. The feeling was surreal – is this finally happening? Suddenly this was more than an idea, more than something I was "going" to do, more than a crazy mid-life fantasy. I would get on a plane in Boston and get off in Oregon with just Crazy Horse to get me home.

As I've said, I'm fortunate to have a tremendous network of friends. This journey never could have happened without them. Mentally and logistically I couldn't have pulled it off by myself. Both dimensions are equally important. Mentally it was important to have the support. My close friends expressed no doubt I could accomplish this task. Did they secretly worry and doubt? Most likely, that they never expressed it was empowering. Logistics was equally important. Keeping an eye on my house and pets was huge. Having someone who could access my office and help if a work emergency arose was also a relief. One of the biggest things was getting me to Oregon and getting me rolling. My friend Beth accompanied me and was a huge help. I never could have coordinated getting a rental car from Portland to Florence and moving my gear around by myself. Plus, it was just nice to have someone with me – I was excited and SCARED.

June 28, 2018, D-Day, arrived with the alarm sounding at 4:45 a.m. The car would pick us up at 5:30 for the ride to Logan Airport in Boston. I was carrying a knapsack and one pannier, everything else had been shipped with the bike. It was a quiet ride to the airport. A little gloomy, overcast and drizzling, still dark at that hour. We got checked in and waited at the gate with coffee and a muffin. Beth's son called; he was a having a dog emergency. He'd recently moved to Florida and was helping the beagle rescue league in Tampa housing dogs waiting for adoption. He'd let his current charge out into the yard where it had an encounter with a poisonous toad! The calls back and forth kept our minds off our journey while we waited for the flight! (The dog survived though it was touch and go for a bit.)

From Jude's Jargon

6/29/2018:

Got into Portland at 12:00 PDT, picked up the rental car and headed south to Florence, OR. It's a small town of about 8,500 right on the coast. The drive from Portland was so beautiful. The country is just VAST. We veered off the main highway and cut over to the coast. Winding roads with the tallest pine trees I've seen anywhere. We knew we were nearing the coast, though, the terrain hadn't changed, still mountainous and forested. Suddenly we came out of the shade and were practically on the beach, ironically in Newport, OR. There were souvenir and surf shops dotting the street. The transformation was spectacular.

We turned south down the Oregon Pacific Coast Highway toward Florence, about 50 miles from Newport. I figured I should call the bike shop to make sure the bike was there. I had emailed "Tim" at Bicycles 101 in Florence a couple of times to tell him I was shipping the bike out. I got one response: "Yes we do that, $100." Last week off went Crazy Horse to the great unknown and to Tim, last name unknown. I had called on Wednesday to see if she had arrived only to get the shop's voicemail saying they were closed Wednesdays. Thursday, I got on the plane having no idea if my bike was there or not. When I phoned from Newport the call was picked up on the third ring "I bet you're wondering if your bike's here." was the first thing I heard. "Well yeah!!!!" "It's here, just finishing up, she's ready to go." "Great, how long will it take us to get down there?" "If you speed, and you should, about an hour." "When do you close?" "Five minutes after you get here." "On the way!"

43

Speeding was not an option! Winding, precarious roads bordered by steep cliffs down to the Pacific. You would wind through the tall pines and come into a clearing with a steep drop and a spectacular view of the ocean. It was not for the faint of heart. We eventually got to the shop and met Tim. Definitely an interesting character! He sells bikes and guitars and has owned the shop for 20 years. There was my Crazy Horse, ready to go as promised. Phew!

Those few days getting ready in Florence were a mixture of apprehension, preparation, and relaxation. After picking up the bike, we made our way to the hotel and unloaded my gear. It was close to six o'clock Pacific time, and we'd been up and going since 5:30 EDT! We cleaned up and headed down to the hotel restaurant to get a bite to eat and a drink. The hotel was right on the ocean, and our room had a balcony overlooking the beach. It was beautiful, the restaurant overlooked the beach too. We sat at the bar and chatted with the guy sitting next to us. Looking as if he'd come from the golf course, I asked if he was a pro. "No, but I played this afternoon." Retired but not much older than me, he explained that he was a Californian and had sold his business and property and moved up to Oregon a few years ago. That would become a familiar theme throughout our stay in Florence and throughout the western states.

The next day we got up early as our bodies were still on East coast time. It was beautiful out, sunny, clear and cool. We found a great spot for breakfast and then explored the town some. Florence is quaint with a population of around 8,000, mostly retirees. It sits on the Siuslaw River and was historically a fishing port. After poking around, we headed to the store to pick up a few supplies for the ride. I didn't get too much as I wanted to keep things light and, frankly, I didn't know what I needed or wanted. This was a whole new experience; I had no idea what to expect. I was getting anxious.

We returned to the hotel, and my anxiety level grew. I figured I should pack my panniers and determine what worked best and make sure my bike was ready to go. As far as packing went, it was difficult. Pete had made sure I had everything I needed for the ride. The problem was, never having done this, I couldn't be sure what I would need and when. It took time to sort all that out. This would also be the first time I would ride with the front panniers because the rack hadn't come in until the day before I shipped the bike. That only added to the stress.

As I went through my tools and equipment, I tried out the portable pump. I should have done this BEFORE I got to Oregon! I pulled it out and was trying to work it, but something just didn't seem right, the valve just didn't fit, and I lost all the air from my front tire without pumping it up. Poor Beth, I was a wreck and angry with frustration. Your tires are about the most important thing and keeping them properly inflated makes a huge difference. If my pump didn't work, I was in a heap of trouble. I took the front tire off, and we got back in the car to see if Tim could help. I was stressed to the max. We got there as he and his buddy were heading out to lunch. "Tim, don't go I need your help!" I implored. He looked a little irritated but looked at the pump and said the connection piece to the valve wasn't there. He showed me one he had in stock and the difference. I bought a new one and felt a little better, still nervous but better! I texted Pete and told him about the issue. He said the valve connector for the one I had brought with me was inside and I had to unscrew the tube to get it and attach it. Duh! There it was just like he said. I felt like a complete and total idiot. Ultimately, the one I bought from Tim was easier to use so I was happier in the long run.

We relaxed for the rest of the afternoon and headed out to dinner in the evening. There was a great little restaurant, The Waterfront Depot, right on the river and jamming that night. We waited for a couple of seats at the bar for my last dinner before the trip. I was anxious but excited to get going. We talked about the plan for the morning. I wanted to get going around 8:00 a.m. Beth would drive my bags to the hotel in Eugene and then head on to the airport to catch her flight out. I was happy to have the first day with no bags. It was 75-80 miles and having never ridden that far before the less weight, the better!

It was a lovely evening, and we chatted with two women sitting next to us out for a "girl's night." They were cute. Being both local and retired, they tried to get out together every so often and leave their husbands at home. We told them they were the first true "locals" we had met; most were California transplants. "Oh yes," they replied. "We call them the Californicators!" There was no love lost there. They explained that the Californians retired and sold off their property and moved up to Oregon to live a cheaper life. However, "cheaper" in terms of California meant that they bought up all the property in the hills along the coastline and built huge houses the natives could never dream of affording. I understood seeing that Westerly, RI often seems like a Connecticut suburb judging by the license plates in town.

After dinner, it was back to the hotel and sleep to prepare for the start of the journey. Would I even be able to sleep?

FINALLY HEADED EAST

I did sleep well that night but was out of bed at 6:30, brimming with nervous energy. I flitted about the room making sure everything was packed correctly. Packing and repacking until it seemed just right, though at this point I still had no idea what "just right" meant. I was ready and anxious, waiting as Beth got her stuff together. Even though I had 80 miles to ride, my day may have been easier than what she was in for. After breakfast, she was driving on to Eugene to drop my bags off at the hotel, then driving up to Portland to drop the car off and catch a flight to San Francisco. From San Fran, she'd be getting on a red eye to Tampa, Fl. to meet her son and husband for the 4th of July holiday. Good friends are hard to find!

Once she was ready, we loaded up the car. I had to do the "tire in the ocean" photo required on any coast to coast ride. That was easier said than done. It was super low tide, so the water was over a quarter mile out through soft sand. I only went halfway out. The ocean behind me would have to be enough! Once that was done, we got Crazy Horse in the car, said good bye to the hotel and headed for breakfast.

We went to the Little Brown Hen, where we had
gone the previous day. It was quite good. Too bad we
weren't sticking around all day because they had some
excellent brunch cocktails on the menu! I was almost too
nervous to eat. The day was finally here. After all the
planning and contemplating it was happening. Thoughts
barreled through my head. "Could I do this?" "Those hills
I've been looking at for the past few days are daunting, and
they're not even close to what I would face in the next few

weeks." "Could my body handle this?" These were all questions for which I had no answer.

We finished, and I made the last pit-stop before departure. It was about 8:30 a.m. and a picture-perfect day. There wasn't a cloud in the sky and brisk there on the coast. That would change quickly as I moved inland, I think it got up to 90 degrees by the time I got to Eugene.

I got Crazy Horse out of the car and made sure I had what I needed for the day. It was a little weird not having the panniers on for that first day. They contained everything I would live on for the next two months, clothes, tools, toiletries, medication, maps, etc. The thought of it being just me and the bike thousands of miles from home was slightly unnerving even if it was only for one day.

It was time to get going. Beth and I said our goodbyes, I hopped on Crazy Horse and set off. I pedaled out of the parking lot and up Rte. 101 for a couple of blocks before turning east on Rte. 126 toward Eugene and, of course, Providence. It was so beautiful, the hills ahead of me and the Siuslaw River flowing along on my right. After a few minutes, Beth drove by and waved. I returned the wave as she pulled away up the road. Now I was truly on my own, just me and the bike and 3,800 miles to go.

Those first few miles that first day were exhilarating. I have always been someone who gets energy and clarity being out in nature by myself. Whether it's a walk through the woods on a crisp fall day, skiing in January, going for a run at dawn or playing a few holes of golf as the sun sets on a perfect summer day. I always feel more alive and closer to whatever spiritual beings are in the universe. However, this day was beyond anything I'd ever experienced before, the energy was immense. Perhaps it was the realization of some subliminal dream or the excitement of embarking on this journey I'd thought so much about. Maybe it was the thrill of not knowing what was around the next bend or the phenomenal beauty of it all. Whatever it was, it was awesome!

From Jude's Jargon:

Day One in the Books!

June 30, 2018

So, it begins! All the planning and thinking and waiting is over with, 80 miles on day one. Yesterday was tough, very anxious and ready to get going. The only other time I can compare it to, and my lawyer friends will get this, is the day before taking the bar exam. You're hyped up and ready to go. You really can't study or prepare any more, and you just want to get started. It was relaxing to get on the bike today!

I couldn't have asked for a more perfect day to start - mid-70's no humidity, not a cloud in the sky. I was also fortunate that I did not have to carry any gear so could get some good miles in on day one. My friend Beth flew out with me to help with the logistics. I never could have gotten this part done without having her here. Flying into Portland and driving several hours, getting my bike squared away and then getting the car back to Portland. She drove ahead to Eugene this morning, checked me into the hotel and dropped off my gear. Can never thank her enough! I was fortunate in that regard and the route wasn't too tough. I stayed on the North Fork of the Siuslaw River most of the way. It wound between the steep hills - so I avoided a lot of climbs!

It was such a cool ride very winding and twisty with little traffic. At times I was literally on roads carved into the sides of hills, steep grade up on my left and an equally steep slope down to the river on the right. The only sound was the river running over the rocks. Truly spectacular. Only one real climb that took me up to 1000 feet. Good practice for the coming days when I get up into 4000-5000 feet of elevation. The ride down the other side of that hill was awesome, I would estimate going 30-35 mph. Fun! Got into Eugene at about 75 miles, the hotel is in Springfield, east of the city, which tacked on another five. Oh well, five less tomorrow!

For those of you who think I'm crazy, I discovered I am nowhere near as crazy as some folks out there. I stopped at a little market in Deadwood, about 30 miles in, for a snack and chatted with the clerk. He said they get lots of cyclists coming through as it's near the beginning (or end) of Adventure Cycling's Trans-America Trail. He said they are usually on their last few legs and coming from the east, he was surprised when I said I had just started today. He told me about one girl finishing her tour. She hadn't just done the United States but started in Australia and had done all the continents! Now that's crazy, though he then told me about a couple even crazier than that. They were finishing the Trans-America but had done it on UNICYCLES! Seriously unicycles - remember there are no free-wheels on those - you pedal 100% of the time - up hills and down! That's not just crazy that's looney tunes!

Well, I'm off to get some food and get ready for Day Two!

That first day wasn't without a few hiccups, however. Eighty miles was further than I'd ever ridden, and I tired over the last 10-15 miles. It had grown hot, and my body was feeling it. I hadn't stopped for a full lunch and had just snacked along the way. That was a mistake, I was running out of energy the closer I got to Eugene. With my blood sugar getting low, I was also getting aggravated and just wanted to be done for the day. This became a pattern throughout the journey. On days I did longer rides, 80 miles or more, the last 10-15 miles would not be fun. You tell yourself that your almost done with just a few miles to go, but you still must ride those miles. That distance would take at least an hour, longer because you're tired after already riding over 80 miles. It became a battle of will, "just keep going" became my mantra. It was frustrating because you just wanted to be done.

When I got to the hotel, I was psyched, only minutes to a hot shower! I wheeled Crazy Horse into the lobby of the Holiday Inn and went up to the desk. Not sure if the room was in my name or Beth's, I gave them mine. That wasn't it, so I had the clerk check for Beth's. He said nope, nothing under that name either. I panicked a little and explained that my bags should be here, and Beth had checked me in earlier. "Sorry not this hotel but maybe it's the Holiday Inn around the corner." Phew, I thought, that's a relief. I rode down the street and found the other hotel, thankfully it was literally around the corner.

I went into the lobby and tried to check in. The clerk said, "nothing under those names here." Now I was pissed on top of being hot, tired and hungry. I said there has to be a reservation, my friend already checked me in, and my bags should be here. I got on the phone and called Beth. "What are you talking about?? I checked you in and dropped off the bags!" She got on the phone with the clerk. Nope, he could find nothing, and my bags weren't there either. Back into panic mode, I shuffled back to the first Holiday Inn. Exasperated, I approached the first clerk again. Explained that my stuff wasn't at the other hotel and they didn't have my bags. Another clerk emerged from the back and heard what was going on, "oh yes," she said, "I think your stuff is here." She found the bags in the closet behind the desk, and the two figured out there was a misspelling on the reservation. Success, at last, my shower was mere minutes away!

I loaded up the bike and headed to the elevators. I discovered one of the hardest things I would have to deal with during the trip was navigating the loaded bike through hotels and elevators. It was awkward and heavy which led to many scrapes and bruises! Finally, into the room and my shower. It became clear after showering that the stress and angst of the day's ride would be washed off along with the dirt and sweat. It was remarkable how much better I would feel each day once I got to my destination, showered and relaxed.

After getting settled and dressed, I headed out to the restaurant down the street from the hotel. I sat at the bar for a beer and some food. The Red Sox were on TV – what could be better! The beer was icy cold, and the food was awesome. A perfect ending to my first day on the road.

HEADING TO THE MOUNTAINS

I was up early and ready to go the next day. I wasn't sure how I would feel after a long day yesterday, but I was fine and ready for day two. It was a shorter day, 45 miles, because day three would take me into the Cascades and up McKenzie Pass.

From Jude's Jargon:

Breakfast with Charles

July 1, 2018

Got up early this morning and relaxed with a cup of coffee before heading out to breakfast. Packed everything up, this will be my first day fully loaded, about 65 lbs. on top of the weight of the bike, 25 pounds. I figured I'd head over to Denny's a block from the hotel. As I pedaled toward the restaurant, a guy on a bike passed me. He looked a little scraggly and had on one of those day-glo traffic vests. I nodded and kept going. I locked up Crazy Horse at Denny's and got a table near the window so I could keep an eye on her. A couple of minutes later the other rider pulled up and locked his bike up. I knew it would be interesting when he came in and asked the people at the counter if they were "the biker." Well, he finally made his way to me and asked if he could share my table. I declined as he seemed a few bricks short of a load. He said he wanted to tell me about riding around the area. He went over and ate at the counter while I had my breakfast.

He came over as I was finishing and asked where I was headed. I said Nimrod then Sisters. He sat down and told me about all the places I should visit when I go through the area, hot springs, lakes, etc. He talked like a runaway train, eventually taking out an envelope and drawing me maps. Talking about places I could walk in with my bike and find cool stuff that people didn't know about. It became quite a map with squiggles and arrows and names of places. He was odd though genuine. Said he'd been riding around the area for 40 years. The waitress brought the check, and I said I had to go. He asked if he could say a prayer for me and took my hand. He launched into a 30 second rant asking God to pray for me and to see me safely through my travels, quite a roll he was on. I asked if he'd help me top off my tires with air and he gladly accepted. We checked out my map, he pointed out some places he talked about, and then he gave me a smaller version of what he had drawn out on the envelope. I wish I had taken a photo of him, was an interesting encounter.

The rest of the day was much less eventful. Rode out to Nimrod, about 40-45 miles of mostly flat roads. I figured to make it an easy day as tomorrow is about 65 miles and contains the dreaded McKenzie Pass – 5300-foot elevation! I'm staying in a quaint little cabin on the McKenzie River. It's an inn and cabins owned by a couple originally from the Netherlands, Bert and Ellie, very sweet. Bert told me the pass wasn't too bad. He'd done it several times and just said to take it slow and stop at the rest areas, and it shouldn't be bad at all! Going to relax on my cabin deck for the rest of the afternoon and listen to the river roll by.

Charles was harmless, and he meant well. Though he did mention he'd been arrested eight times as he helped me get my tires pumped up. He liked to proselytize in public places which wasn't well received. He was the only person I met on the entire trip who made me even a little uncomfortable. I found that for the most part people were genuinely interested in my journey and were always willing to help with anything I needed.

WHAT WAS I THINKING?

Here I was on my third day into the journey, and I was facing the hardest day. I had spent an inordinate amount of time in the months leading up to the trip thinking about this day. I would try to conquer McKenzie Pass, elevation 5,300 feet. Nothing I had done to train could prepare me for this. It would be the most elevation gain in any one day of the entire trip. I had a few things going for me, fresh legs and naivete! Think about it, I was on the third day of my first bicycle tour, and I had no idea what this challenge would be like. Could I pedal the whole way? Would I make it at all? Would the Pass even be open? It's generally closed from November 1st to the end of June and sometimes into July due to snow cover. This would be an early test of my fortitude.

There were two options to get from Nimrod to Sisters; stay on Rte. 126 and go over Santiam Pass or turn onto Rte. 242 to go over McKenzie Pass. There were pluses and minuses to both. Santiam added 20 miles to the route making it an 85-mile day and had heavier traffic, but the elevation was less. McKenzie was 20 miles shorter, but no trucks allowed, they simply couldn't make the switchback turns required to get up the mountain, but it was a steeper climb. Santiam was only 500' lower in elevation than

McKenzie, so I opted to save the 20 miles! Besides, I was there, and I wouldn't want to look back and tell myself I wimped out!

I started around 7:15 a.m. riding for an hour before breakfast. There were no restaurants in Nimrod, and after making myself the worst spaghetti dinner I'd ever eaten the night before, I felt it necessary to get a good hot breakfast in me before taking on the pass. It was chilly when I started, mid-50's. I was learning to appreciate that as I knew that it would warm up quickly and I would experience temperatures close to ninety on my way up the pass. I wasn't used to the hot, dry air. It was very deceiving coming from the heavy humidity of the northeast.

From Jude's Jargon:

Bent But Not Broken

July 2, 2018

"Wow" is really all I can say about today. I knew the climb would be hard, but this was beyond my expectations. I started early, 7:15 a.m. and rode for about an hour then stopped for breakfast. It would be a 65 mile plus day so better load up. The first 20 miles were uneventful, fairly flat and traffic was light. At the

20-mile mark, I turned off Rte. 126 and onto 242, the "scenic route" which would take me over McKenzie Pass. The best thing about it was trucks are not allowed, so traffic was light the whole way through. People are good about sharing the road with cyclists, though often they don't have a choice as the road gets narrow with switchbacks and 90-degree plus curves.

I took it very easy starting out. It was so quiet with the pines towering over the road and no cars, I was truly by myself. The terrain was gentle and rolling. I thought this wasn't too bad. I hit 2000 feet and then 3000. It got harder, more switchbacks and climbs. I would stop occasionally to catch my breath and rest my legs. As I got closer to 4000 feet it got tough, I'd stop every half mile or so. My legs were shaky as I got out of my pedals. The road was super twisty and every corner I went around brought more uphill. As I was resting at one point, 3-4 guys biked past me, going downhill! I started again, and a few more came down. I thought I was the only idiot going UP the hill! I would ride literally a few hundred yards then rest. My legs would feel good as I began again only to burn out quickly. I was snacking as much as I could, trying to stay ahead of it.

I hit 4000 feet, and that was it, the switchbacks were steep, and I couldn't ride any more. I basically walked my bike up to almost 5000 feet. The landscape changed, which was heartening. No longer were the trees looming above me, I could see beyond them and knew it couldn't get much higher. Things were getting scraggly. There were a few switchbacks where I would get around the corner and literally be 50-100 feet higher than the road below. Talk about steep!

I have pushed myself hard before, but this was beyond anything I've ever done. I was constantly in touch with my body, trying to keep my heart-rate under control, listening to my muscles telling me to rest, continuing to move forward. It was an intense challenge both mentally and physically. Could I do this? There were times I questioned it. Even walking was hard pushing 65 pounds up those hills. The air was thin, "sucking wind" took on an entirely new meaning. Thankfully it was also cooler the higher I got, though I could feel the sweat running down my back.

As I got closer to 5000 feet, it got better. I could get back on the bike and coast down slight hills. I came around a corner to find an amazing lava field. The pictures don't do it justice. It was like being on the moon. I was still walking up hills as the road was narrow and the drop-offs steep with no guardrails. Finally, I came around a corner and saw cars parked - this had to be it! I had done it - reached McKenzie Pass! I must admit it was a rush – there were moments I didn't think I could make it, but suddenly there it was. I was the only cyclist up there. A guy came by and asked which way I had come from - I nodded my head west, and he said: "that's quite a climb." NO KIDDING! Another woman came by and said, "you're my hero of the day!" I asked if it was downhill until Sisters. She replied, "mostly, yes."

I had a serious adrenaline rush and got back on my bike to head down the last 15 miles. It was a surreal scene, much of the terrain had been devastated by fires last year. A wasteland. While my legs didn't have to do much in those 15 miles, though it was hardly an easy ride. Tension shifted to my arms, back and hands. More switchbacks on the way down, I was on the brakes most of the way. Had to stop at one point to stretch out my back and my hands. Thankfully I was riding on the inside as the drop-offs were still steep. I only had to come down about 2000 feet to get into Sisters.

Got to Sisters at 4:00 p.m., more than eight hours after I started. Walked down the street and got a great steak sandwich and a beer...never tasted so good! Tomorrow is another day, and Crazy Horse and I will be ready. Fortunately, a short day 40 miles, and flat!!!

It was a great accomplishment, and I was weary at the finish, but once again the shower washed off the day's stress along with the grime and sweat. As I walked around town checking out the shops and looking for a good place for dinner, I could feel my legs. Even stepping up or down a curb gave my quads and calves little stabs of pain.

Sisters was my first experience with what I deem a true "western town." As I walked down a dirt path from my cabin/motel to the street a pair of prairie dogs popped up and scampered between their tunnels. First time I'd seen a prairie dog! I walked through the parking lot of a vegetable stand and came upon a deer snacking on some food the workers had discarded at the back door. I was not in Providence anymore!

These towns generally consisted of one main street lined with one- and two-story buildings. Sisters was no different. They remind me of the scene from Blazing Saddles where they erect a main street to fool the governor's men into thinking it was the real town. The buildings are all roughly the same height, square and clapboard shingled. It was much the same in every town from there to Fargo.

From Jude's Jargon:

Climate change!

66

July 3, 2018

Today was uneventful, flat 45 miles from Sisters to Prineville, OR. Flat is good after yesterday, though even the slightest incline was an unwelcome sight! Going over the pass was like entering another atmosphere. On the west side lush greenery with towering pines, on the east side almost desert-like with scraggly pine, rocks, and dirt. Tons of ranches, both horse and cattle - even an alpaca ranch!

The territory was expansive with rock mesas along my route. It was beautiful though arid. Great climate for riding. 83 degrees when I reached Prineville, humidity 13%. Had to throw that in for all my friends back home, sorry!

Going to head out to dinner soon...not much to report for the day. Tomorrow another climb on the schedule - Ochoco Pass 4700 feet, however starting from 3000 will be helpful! Hopefully, I'm getting acclimated to the altitude! Then onto to Mitchell, OR population 130, 55 miles in all. Wonder if they will have fireworks for the Fourth?

Hope everyone has a great holiday - Happy Birthday - USA!

I spent that night in Prineville, OR and walked down to the Club Pioneer Restaurant for dinner at the suggestion of the hotel clerk. The bar area was dark and rustic, quiet early on the holiday eve. I sat at the bar sipping my beer and checking out the menu, another woman was sitting a couple stools over chatting with the bartender. A few minutes later two young men in their mid to late 20's came in from the patio. They approached the bar to my left to order drinks. One of them ordered a Long Island Iced Tea and instructed the bartender on which brands of alcohol to use and how to make it. He had a high sing-song voice. I surmised he was gay by his general appearance and attitude. The other young man, dressed in dusty jeans and cowboy boots, quickly ordered a beer. They got the drinks and headed back outside. As they passed us the young man with the beer paused. He looked at the woman next to me and said, "he's my cousin" and kept going. The bartender, also female, the woman and I looked at each other and burst out laughing. "Wow," the woman said, "guess he's a little self-conscious." When they were at the bar, I hadn't thought about them one way or another. I guess it's still hard for a young cowboy to come to grips with homosexuality.

BEST FOURTH OF JULY EVER!

I had never spent the 4th of July outside of New England and not more than a couple outside of Rhode Island so this would be a different experience. It didn't feel like the 4th of July, just another day on the road. The routine was established, get up, eat breakfast at the hotel, get on the bike and go.

Breakfast that day was funny. I went down and got settled with my first bowl of cereal. There was a group of guys sitting around a table. They were motorcycle touring around the area during the holiday week and were all in their mid-60's. As I sat down nearby, I noticed "I Love Lucy" reruns were playing on the TV. I thought little of it. The woman taking care of the breakfast buffet came out to check on things and make sure there was plenty of food and coffee when one guy asked her if she could switch the channel to some news.

"Oh no! There is no news in this room! I've had to listen to too many political fights over the news! We watch 'I Love Lucy.' Period." She exclaimed before retreating to the kitchen just off the dining room. We all chuckled a little and went back to our breakfasts. Another of the motorcyclists came down to join the others. He asked them why the news wasn't, and they told him to go into the kitchen and ask the woman to change the channel. He promptly did so which drew the same response from her. The guys were howling laughing! A couple of minutes later another one came down, and they told him to go ask the woman to put on the news. He didn't hesitate. The same response emanated from the kitchen until she figured it out and emerged laughing and waving her towel at the guys. I made it a point from there on out not to bring up politics in my encounters along the route.

From Jude's Jargon:

Celebrating the 4th in Small-town America

July 5, 2018

I got up early on the 4th and got ready to ride from Prineville to Mitchell, OR, 55 miles. There's a 4,700' climb in the Ochoco Mountains to Ochoco Pass, so I wanted to get an early start and perhaps have a full afternoon in Mitchell. It was a crisp morning in the mid-'60s when I started at 7:45. Traffic was quiet with the holiday; I had the road to myself. It was mostly flat for the first 17 miles or so. I ran into another rider at the foot of the first hill. He was from Eugene and just hopping around and camping for the week. He said the climb wasn't too bad. We talked for a bit and went our separate ways. I took the climb and went up into the Ochoco National Forest. Beautiful winding roads with lots of trees and creeks. It was gentle up and down. At about 35 miles I was suddenly at the top - I couldn't believe it - that seemed like nothing. Particularly after the brutality of McKenzie Pass! I was coming from the right direction as I don't think I pedaled for 12 miles on the way down! It was a little white knuckle at times but not bad. I met another rider on my descent, he was heading up the opposite direction. We chatted for a few minutes. He was coming from Chicago and heading up to Astoria, OR and then down the coast to San Francisco. He had come through Mitchell and said it was a neat little town. I knew it was small as my maps give population. They list Mitchell at 130 people.

I finished the descent and coasted into Mitchell at about 1:00 p.m. I had made a reservation at one hotel the night before. As I came down the main road, Rte. 26 I saw the sign for the "Mitchell Business Loop" so I turned off. Business loop may have been an overstatement. There was a small café, a little gift shop, two gas pumps - not stations, pumps, a small brew pub, and the Oregon Hotel. That was it. My reservation wasn't at the Oregon, but as I passed it, I was compelled to stop and check it out. The front porch was welcoming with some chairs and tables. It was right on the "strip," and clearly, the place where I had reserved was not. I pulled my bike up to the Oregon. By now the temperature had risen into the 90's, and I was glad to be done riding for the day. I walked onto the porch and went in the front door. It was cool and dry in the lobby, though no one was about. The lobby was merely a big room with a small counter by the door. It had a sitting area in front of a fire place with some comfortable chairs. The sign on the door next to the counter said: "Please knock for service." I did as instructed. A moment or two later a young man came out to check me in. As I had no reservation, he had to check the notebook to see if there was a room available. No computer reservations here! He asked if I wanted the first or second floor. I kind of shrugged and he said take the second, it's quieter. Quieter than what??, I said to myself. We chatted for a few minutes, and I discovered his grandparents owned the place, and he would be starting his senior year in high school this fall. He also told me Mitchell was famous because his grandfather owned a bear. "It's on You Tube." He asked where I was from and then informed me that he'd been out of Oregon only twice, once across the

72

border to California for a day or two and then once to Idaho, but he came back the same day. We talked about the 4th of July, and I suggested they probably didn't do much with fireworks due to the fire risk. He proudly said they had some and the fire marshal had given them permission to light them off in the street!

After checking in, he showed me where I could keep my bike as they weren't allowed inside. We went around back, greeted by the family dogs; a bull mastiff, a coonhound mix and a little terrier named Oopsey! They all vied for my attention demanding to be pet. His little brother came over, and they watched me unload the bike. I felt like an alien, though I'm sure they'd seen many bikers before, they seemed curious about my trip. I went up the creaky wooden stairs to find my room, looking forward to a nice shower. The room was sparse, but the bed looked comfy. I set down my bags and headed into the bathroom to shower and, alas, what did I find but an old claw-foot tub - no shower. I laughed and said I guess it's bath time! I got cleaned up and got ready to check out the street. I had no cell service, and the internet was down. That was actually great!

I walked down to the Tiger Town Brewery to get a snack and a beer. It was small, a few tables and four seats at the bar, but busy. I sat at the bar next to a nice couple just out for a holiday drive. We had a nice chat; pensions are a problem in Oregon too. Though "not as bad as in California"! The bartender fit the scene perfectly, 35-40, long beard, Levi's, plaid shirt and vest, and a large buck-knife sheathed across the small of his back! I chatted with him when the couple left. His name was Eric, and he had grown up on a ranch about 20 miles outside of town, he said it was the same for most in the area. He was one of the owners of the brewery, Tiger Town Brewing Co., he managed the restaurant and bar because he "had the prettiest face," one partner brewed the beer and the other was a carpenter of some sort - "he built stuff in the back." Eric was running hard, making sure the food got out, and the drinks were full. He said they'd been in business for a couple of years and were "evolving." The beer was good and so were the wings. He was a little surprised I ordered the "hotter" buffalo wings! I finished the wings and beer and walked the block back to the hotel to sit on the front porch and read. Tremendously relaxing, the whole town just moved at its own pace. A guy parked his truck outside the hotel while I sat there. He greeted me as he walked up the steps and asked if the internet was back up to which I replied yes (apparently the whole town was down) he said "good, I just fixed it." He was deservedly proud.

I sat there for a few hours and took it all in. I figured I should eat some dinner as I had a long ride the next day, so I walked down the street to find the only thing left open was the brewery. I had my second meal of the day there. Eric was still at it working hard. I headed back to the room about 8:00 to read and get ready for sleep. Read for a while then contemplated the town. It had its heyday in the late 19th and early 20th centuries when the miners were flocking from the east. It had been entirely wiped out a couple of times via fire or flood yet hung on. That was the spirit. People worked hard and played hard all just trying to survive! It was a beautiful way to spend the fourth, no traffic, no big events, just people being Americans. As I drifted off to sleep, I heard the boys lighting off their firecrackers in the street, approved by the fire department, of course.

Though I'd only been riding a few days, it seemed like a long time, perhaps because I was still so far from home and had over 3,500 miles to go. I was almost 300 miles into Oregon as I left Mitchell on the 5th and would spend a few more days in the state. Coming from New England and Rhode Island, in particular, it's just inconceivable to be in one state for so long! That lent to the feeling I was farther into the journey than I was.

As I got further east things became sparser and I had to pay more attention to the distances between the places I would stop for the night. Services were getting fewer and farther between. While I had camping gear with me, the last thing I wanted to do was ride all day then figure out what to eat, how to cook it and then spend the night on the ground in a tent! I'm not a big fan of camping anyway, so the above scenario held no glamour. I had the gear with me, if I got stuck anywhere, but was reconsidering keeping it due to the added weight.

The morning of the 5th I headed out of Mitchell early on route to John Day about 70 miles to the east. I was still in the Ochoco Mountains and had to get over Keyes Creek Pass about 7 miles into the day. The weather was messing with my head because the days would start clear and somewhat cool, in the high 50's, but by noon the temperatures would creep up into the 90's. I focused on the destination so I wouldn't notice how hot it was until I stopped for a break. Because the dry, arid climate was so different from the muggy humidity of New England in the summer, I wasn't used to it. It just didn't feel as hot as it was. There was only one town between Mitchell and John Day, Dayville about 35 miles into the ride, so I knew I had a place to grab lunch.

This stretch was nice, beautiful country with little traffic. It was the day I discovered snakes like to curl up in the road to get warm on the pavement. I went by one and didn't realize at first it was alive. I went by a couple more, and one moved as I passed. The next one I spotted saw me and gave a nice hiss! I didn't slow down or get close enough to see whether they were rattlesnakes, but the patterns of their skin matched photos I'd seen! It was a good thing I spotted them because it made me more cognizant when I pulled off the road to stop and rest for a few minutes. I always did a quick scan to make sure there weren't any around!

When I got to about five or six miles out of Dayville, I came upon an accident. The road was winding, and you couldn't see far ahead as you went. A box truck had flipped over and was off the right side of the road. Another motorist had stopped and parked about fifty yards before the truck to slow people down as they came around the curve. The driver of the truck sat on a rock next to the truck. He was holding a rag against his bloody head. He seemed okay but for the gash and they had things under control, so I kept going.

I got to Dayville and settled into a booth next to a window at the local café. As I perused the menu, a state trooper went flying by toward the accident. I couldn't believe it, it had to be thirty minutes since I passed the accident. There was no doubt about where the trooper was going because there were no other roads around. I was astonished at how long it had taken him to get out there, I was so used to city life where emergency responders arrived within minutes of an accident.

From Jude's Jargon:

I left Mitchell on the 5th after my relaxing 4th of July and headed to John Day, 70 miles to the east. The day started off with a serious climb to Keyes Creek Pass, 4,369. It was my sixth consecutive day in the saddle, and I was feeling it. I needed to hike the last mile and push Crazy Horse to the top. There was a road crew working on the shoulder, and we chatted for a few minutes while I passed. They gave me the lowdown on what was ahead and wished me luck. Thankfully it was a beautiful descent once over the top. I still had 63 miles to go, the day was nowhere near over. I was still in high desert country so a

78

smattering of ranches and mostly barren hills. One stretch took me through Picture Gorge where the road winds through steep hills along the John Day River. It was beautiful and flat. I got to Dayville for lunch and wolfed down a milkshake, roast beef sandwich, and fries. Unfortunately, it was getting hot, and I still had 35 miles to go. I'm finding that the last 10 miles of each day isn't fun. You know you're close, but still 45 minutes to an hour out, you're tired, "hangry" and just want to be done. I got into John Day around 4:00 p.m. It was 97 degrees. I was ready for a day off, and I took it. Got laundry done and just hung around. Didn't feel great, think the previous day's heat did a number on me. One cool thing happened though. Okay, all you Rumford natives, this one's for you - at noon the whistle blew! Raise your hand if you remember the noon whistle from Rumford Baking Powder!

My first day off was uneventful, spent it in John Day. I did pull the plug on the camping gear. It was just too much weight for something I didn't want to use anyway. I found a post office and shipped it all home – 11 lbs. As I walked to dinner that night, I saw deer running across the main street. It was a mom, dad and a couple of fawns passing through, perhaps they were on a family outing to find a good place for dinner!

79

The next day I set out for a long day going from John Day to Baker City.

From Jude's Jargon:

While having dinner that night (in John Day) I met Gunther and Hans from Munich, Germany. They run 3-4 motorcycle tours a year for Europeans through the U.S. Very interesting guys. They and their group were staying at my hotel. It was too funny when I left my room in the morning to head out, they were organizing for their day's ride. Gunther called me over and introduced me to the group. He explained what I was doing. However, he told them in German. I had no idea what he was saying, but there were a lot of raised eyebrows as they had just ridden the same route but in reverse. You will see it's not easy!

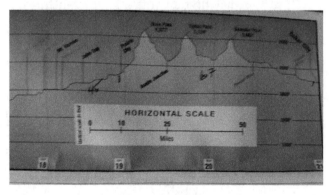

I set out early that morning. I knew it would not be a fun day and I wanted to catch the cool part of the day. Check out the map - John Day to Baker City, three climbs, 80 miles! The day off really helped. I felt fresh, and my legs were good. The first fifteen or so miles were easy, yet I was trying to conserve as much as I could and coasting on every downhill. I made the first two climbs with plenty of water breaks along the way. I'd have to stop every mile or so to catch my breath and rest. My mile split times dropped from 11-12 mph to 4-5 on the ascents then once over the top they'd increase to 20-25 mph. I was usually on the brakes as the descents are steep and winding. Very tense, making sure the bike stays under control. I did have to walk up the last mile of the third climb, my legs were toast, and I still had 27 miles to go. Once off the steep descent, it was a nice ride until turning north to head into Baker City. For the last 10 miles, I had a strong headwind. Really??? This has to happen now??? It was not fun!

That morning, not far out of John Day, I met another cyclist also heading east. It was around 9:30 a.m. when I came up on him stopped on the side of the road. We were just heading into the hills with the climbs. The first words out of his mouth were, "It's been a long day." I looked at him a little funny and said: "it's only like 9:30 in the morning." He said, "I know, but I've been riding for 22 hours straight." My jaw hit the pavement. Why would anyone do that, I thought to myself, these roads were tricky in the daylight, never mind during the night!

He was young, probably 23-24, and was traveling light. He explained that he was from Maryland and his hobby was doing endurance training and competing in ultra-endurance events. There's a race every spring which goes from Astoria, Oregon to Yorktown, Va. called the Trans-America because it follows the Adventure Cycling Association's Trans-America Trail. He had missed the race this year but wanted to get ready for next year. I said "what are you riding? Like 12 hours a day?" He said he was shooting for sixteen but had fallen behind so was making up time. He wanted to finish in 20 days, the winners do it in around 17 days! It's 3,200 miles...in 17 days! I had been on the road for 8 days and managed only 380 miles, let that sink in for a minute! Granted I would make up time and miles once I got out of the mountains but seriously 17 days! People thought I was crazy to take this on, but this goes to show that everyone has their own level of crazy!

I made it the rest of the way to Baker City, but it was not a fun day. It was rather grueling, three passes to go over, all over 5,000' and steep at the top. Then I dealt with some serious headwinds over the last 10 miles on the way into town. I found my motel for the night, the Oregon Motel and Restaurant, and checked in. After a nasty, exhausting day of riding where was my room? On the second floor! Elevator? Of course not! So, I lugged all my bags up then Crazy Horse. Three separate trips my legs screaming on every stair.

I cleaned up, the magical shower wiping away the travails of the day and thought about dinner. The motel restaurant would be the easiest, but it didn't look too appealing and didn't have booze, so it was not an option. I was looking forward to a cold beer after a long, hot day! I walked a few blocks and found a nice bar/restaurant. As was my habit, I grabbed a seat at the bar so I could chat with whoever was around. It was Saturday night around six, and not much was going on. There were a few tables full, but it was otherwise quiet. Two young guys were hanging at the bar having shots and beers. They were kicking their night off and knew the bartenders (female). We chatted for a bit, and they were on their way, after inviting the bartenders to a party later. The last thing on my mind was a party. I had a couple of very cold beers and a French dip with fries and headed back to the motel to get ready for another day in the saddle.

LAST DAY IN OREGON

I got up the next morning raring to go, it was my last day in Oregon. I'd be into Idaho tomorrow. Had breakfast at the motel restaurant which reaffirmed my choice not to have dinner there the night before. It was fine for breakfast, but dinner would be a stretch. After breakfast and lugging my bike and bags back down the stairs I was off to Halfway, OR.

From Jude's Jargon:

Today's ride was a little shorter, 55 miles, though a serious climb during the final 13 miles. The beginning was nice. Went through more plains surrounded by mountains. Really beautiful. Came across a few more snakes in the road but didn't slow down to discover what kind they were or take a photo! I got to Richland, 42 miles, in 3 hours, the next thirteen would take an hour and a half! I fueled up and rested for a half hour before taking on the rest of the ride. I was sitting outside the market when a couple drove up and parked. The woman asked if I was heading toward Halfway. When I told her, "yes," she sighed, "that's a tough one 7% grade for about

4 miles." Oh, joy! The country was wide open in front of me, and I could see the climb ahead of me, two long inclines with switchbacks. I started up but knew I wouldn't make it too long before having to push the bike. Pushed her for the last 3 miles with lots of breath catching and water breaks! Once again the temperature was in the mid-90's. Finally, I crossed the top, and it was downhill to Halfway!

As I rode into town, there was a rodeo going on at the fairgrounds, a junior rodeo. Instead of soccer, lacrosse and field hockey tournaments, the parents cart their kids around to compete in rodeos on weekends! After I cleaned up and checked into my room, I headed back out to the rodeo. It was a full-on rodeo complete with bull riding! They do start them young. Kids were riding around the infield on the horses, complete with cowboy hats and spurs! It was a great way to end the day. Off to dinner now and to rest up for Hells Canyon tomorrow!

From Jude's Jargon:

Hells Canyon and the Kindness of Strangers July 7, 2018

"Whoever you are, I have always depended on the kindness of strangers." Blanche DuBois, A Streetcar Named Desire. It was an interesting day, had a few "firsts." One, I've never been to Idaho, so check that box, and, two I've never hitchhiked, check that one too. Now before all my police, prosecutor and judicial friends get all wound up, hear me out! Most of you know my background, cop, prosecutor, defense attorney, etc., etc. etc. I've seen people at their worst and at their best. I am inclined to believe that most people are generally "good." I know those of you whose lives are steeped in crime and criminals would beg to differ, but I do believe that. Think about the chances of some lurking predator happening to be on the sparsely traveled road in Idaho I happened to be on at noon today, you might as well play the lottery or hope to get struck by lightning - the odds may be better!

I started the morning from Halfway, OR at about 7:45 a.m. It was lovely, 65 degrees, though I knew the temps would climb significantly throughout the day and that I would be going through Hells Canyon which averages 10-20 degrees warmer than the surrounding towns. The first 40 miles were uneventful and pleasant, mostly downhill with little to no traffic. I had to laugh when I came upon the pictured sign. Congestion?? Does someone have a cold? I cannot possibly imagine there has ever been anything close to a traffic jam on this road! I got to Oxbow and turned off toward the Snake River and Idaho. I came around a corner and happened upon a reservoir. I had to stop and do a double take. The water was so serene it took me a moment to determine I was looking at a reflection of the surrounding hills. Quite spectacular. I got to the Brownlee Dam which is the crossover into Idaho. It was gorgeous. The road "snaked" along the river which was a good half mile wide, crystal clear and glass calm. Turned off the river and into the canyon. Stopped at a market/café to add some hydration as I knew I was about to hit the climb, 6 miles 2,100'. to 4,100' elevation, 7-8% grade. Once I hit the hill, I started pushing Crazy Horse, faster than trying to ride it. Plus, it was likely 110 degrees.

After about a mile I said to myself, "this is stupid, it's going to take a couple of hours for me to get up this thing" and heat stroke was not on my agenda for the day! I heard a car coming up behind me and out went the thumb! It was a pick-up, thankfully, though the chances were high. The driver pulled over and stuck his head out. "Can I catch a ride to the top?" "Sure." He got out and helped me get my bike in the bed. A young guy, in his late 20's. He declared that I was not the first person he'd given a ride up the canyon. We chatted on the short ride. He lives a couple of miles from where he picked me up but was selling his property and starting his own business, pipe fitting, and welding. He said he was trying to close on the property but was worried about capital gains. Someone had mentioned a 10-something to him. I

89

said "1031 exchange?" "Yeah, that's it!" I told him it was a tax law and he should talk to a lawyer or accountant. He said, "I wish they taught that stuff in high school." So, a little free legal advice for a 10-minute ride that saved me hours! A good bargain! We got to the top, and he said he was going onto Cambridge, which is where I am staying for the night. He could bring me all the way in. I passed - can't cheat that much! We shook hands after getting my bike out of the truck. "Taylor," he said, "good to meet you." "Judy, likewise." He drove off down the hill.

I got back on the bike and headed toward town. About 10 minutes later I stopped to flip over my map and get a drink when a sheriff pulled up. "You doing okay?" I told him yes and that I'd gotten a ride up the canyon. "Do you have plenty of water?" Yup, all set. Very thoughtful I decided. When I got into town, I pulled up in front of a mini-mart to get the directions to the B&B where I'm staying when another truck pulled up. A man got out of the driver's side and went inside. The woman in the passenger seat leaned out and told me I shouldn't be out riding on a day like today! "I'm done for the day!" I declared. "Good," she said, "it's too hot to be out here on a bike." Yet another concerned and, by the way, nice person.

So that's my tale of random acts of kindness. Yes, most people are nice, at least all those I've come across so far on this adventure. Now I'm tucked away in my room for the night - resting up for tomorrow's adventure. Did I mention that when I got in Taylor's truck there was a 9mm on the console and a shotgun wedged between my seat and the console??? Felt safe riding with him - for real!

From Jude's Jargon:

What Time Is It????

July 8, 2018

I passed into Idaho and into the Mountain time zone over 100 miles ago. This morning I headed out of Riggins, ID at about 8:00 a.m. I rode for about an hour, 13 miles or so, and came upon a sign reading "Pacific Time Zone." What? I've been in Mountain time for over a day now, and suddenly I'm back to Pacific. Sure enough, my phone now said 8:06 a.m. Does this negate the 13 miles I just rode? When will I be back in Mountain time? When I get to today's destination, Grangeville 50 miles out? This was weird, I've been going north - northeast to get to Missoula and apparently when I get into Montana it goes

91

back to Mountain time. I had to ask the clerk at the hotel what zone I was in, she confirmed Pacific. The events of the ride had taken over, and I couldn't remember where I was when it changed and if it had changed back.

The last two days have been difficult, perhaps why I couldn't figure out what time it is. Yesterday started great. Had breakfast at the B&B I stayed at in Cambridge with the owner. She'd opened the place a couple of years prior. She wanted to do something for herself. She and her husband own and farm 1,200 acres about 70 miles from Cambridge. They grow wheat, sugar beets, onions and of course potatoes. I will wonder this winter when I order spuds whether they originated at her farm. Mid-summer is slow until harvest, so she figured she'd open the inn, though she's never even stayed at a B&B herself! She says it's been great she's learned a lot about people and a lot about herself.

After breakfast, I set off for Riggins, ID 80 miles out. I had a 1,400' climb, but it was gradual over the first fifty miles. I figured the last thirty would be great as it was downhill all the way into Riggins. I stopped for a snack in New Meadows then headed out toward Riggins. Had to make a left turn to stay on the route. Unfortunately, it turned me directly into the wind, and it was not just a gentle breeze, but 10-15 mph. It kept me on the bike for at least an extra hour. Going down hills which I would normally do 18-20+ mph I was down to 12-14. It was brutal, I was tired and "hangry." I could feel the wind burning my face. It was miserable. For those of you who wonder why I'm doing this by myself, you would not have wanted to be in my company last evening! I got to the motel a beautiful spot right on the Salmon River. A gentleman was sitting in the lobby with a black lab which looked like it had been for a recent swim. We chatted for a minute. He said you should go for a swim - the temperature of the river is perfect. Boy did that sound good. He continued to say there was a great spot with a little beach about a mile down. The mile thing killed it for me! I'd been on the road for 9 hours, and all I wanted was food and bed!

Woke up hungry this morning even though I'd eaten a small pizza last night! Grabbed breakfast at the motel and set out. There were two possibilities for the day. Try to push it and go for 85 miles so I could get to Missoula on Friday. My niece and a friend are flying in from L.A. for the weekend so want to spend some time with them. 85 today would ensure that, but it would depend on the day and my legs. The other alternative was to go fifty and stop in Grangeville, do a quick forty tomorrow and then have two days to get through the final 120 to Missoula on Saturday.

The day started nice, cool about 55, and the ride was good. Light traffic and flat or down hill for the first 30, then I got to White Bird and the climb of the day. It had taken about 2.5 hours to get to White Bird, that pace was about to change drastically. The climb is a 7% grade over 8.5 miles - yikes! I rode about a mile up the hill, and it got steeper. Time to walk. Switched into sneakers and started pushing Crazy Horse. I made it about 4 miles, stopping every three quarters of a mile to rest and drink. Averaging about 3 mph. Good news, no cars on the road, bad news, no cars on the road. I stopped as I was approaching a long, steep incline to have a snack and some water, hoping that someone in a pick-up would come by. My legs were dying. Finally, after about a half

94

hour an ancient pick was coming down the hill. I waved for him to stop. "I know you're going down, but do you think you could bring me to the top?" "Sure, let me go turn around." "Thank you, thank you, thank you!" I honestly am not sure I could have hiked up the last 4 miles.

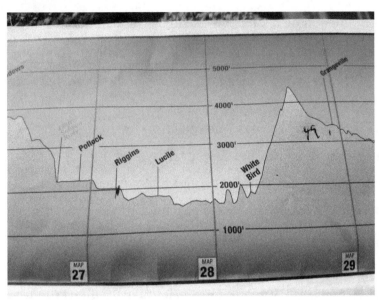

When I suggested the pick-up was "ancient" I wasn't kidding. I came to find out it was an '87 Dodge Ram. The only thing new in it was the pesticide he'd just picked up in Grangeville and the obligatory topless dashboard calendar from the local body shop, accurate in July 2018. We put the bike in the back and got in. My savior was a local rancher, Jerry Stiles, a.k.a. Moose. He was on his way back to White Bird after running errands.

The truck groaned its way up the hill, probably sounded like me pushing Crazy Horse. Man was it steep! I was on the outside, and all I could do was look down into the ravine and hope the truck would make it. No guardrails, precarious. Moose told me some about the area and dropped me at the top of the hill. I might still be out there if he hadn't come along! A nice smooth downhill and I was in Grangeville, there would be no going on today - wind is up again, and my body simply said, "no"!

Since my return, one question I get asked continuously is whether I ever felt scared during the trip. To be honest, the scariest thing I encountered was the trucks, particularly the logging trucks in Oregon, Idaho, and Montana. I was mostly traveling on two lane roads that often had little in the way of shoulders. The loggers have no love loss for cyclists. They wouldn't give an inch when passing me by, often at speeds of 60-70 miles per hour. Even if there was no other traffic on the road and they could move over to give me some room they refused. I would hear them coming up behind me and immediately tense up – which is about the worst thing you can do. I'd hang on for dear life as they whizzed by, all the while wondering if this was my day to die. It was nerve racking. Depending on where I was and how tired I was I often opted to pull off the road entirely while they passed me by.

It was worth losing a little time to gain some peace of mind. It was also tough when they came by from the opposite direction. Once they passed, the backdraft would hit you square in the face, again you'd have to hold on tight. This was particularly troubling when going downhill with some speed. With the bike being loaded, the wind plus the weight could easily send you off the road. Remember, guardrails seem optional out there! Once I got beyond to that part of the country, the truckers were very courteous and generally gave me a wide berth.

As for people, I never once felt threatened throughout the journey. Even my proselytizing, cycling enthusiast, acquaintance Charles from Eugene, though odd, was harmless. As the stories I've related prove, most people were exceptionally friendly, interested in what I was doing and my experiences. One morning in Council, ID I had stopped to get a drink and was standing outside the store with my bike. An older woman walked up and after giving me and the bike the once over said: "How old are you?" Not "hi" or "how are you," just right to the point. I told her I was fifty-two and she said, "Okay I guess that's young enough to be doing this." That was our whole conversation. She was so cute. Most offered to help any way they could and were happy to talk about their own lives and experiences. As you will see further along in the journey, people are very willing to share very personal things with total strangers. Maybe I should have been a bartender because people just seem to like to unload on me.

INCOMMUNICADO

During the months leading to the trip my friends and family expressed concern about knowing where I would be. Sometimes it seemed a little much, but it was nice they were worried. My friend Kathy wanted to implant a GPS chip in my body so I could be located anywhere, that might have been a bit much. I wasn't worried about it before I left. I did acquiesce and found an app called Glimpse that allowed me to share my location with select people. It was perfect because I could set it for a certain amount of time. If it were a long day on the road, I would set it for 8-10 hours. I only had to click on the contacts I wanted to see it, and they could follow me in real time. The last thing I would do before starting the day is turn on the app. From what I've heard since being back a few people may have been a little addicted to checking on me all the time,

I'd had no problem with cell connectivity, and most places had wifi, so I wasn't thinking much about it when I left Grangeville and headed for Lowell, ID. It was a short 47-mile hop, and I would travel through the Nez Perce Indian Reservation for much of it. Grangeville is a large town, population about 3,200, so I had all the services in the hotel that night. Think I stayed at a Best Western.

It was another beautiful day; I hadn't seen a drop of rain in almost two weeks on the road. I headed out and quickly learned why the town was called Grangeville. I rode through acres of farms, mostly corn. The road was gently rolling so I could see for miles. I may have seen one or two cars all morning as I rode through the reservation. While in Grangeville and the immediately surrounding area, I had been on a plateau. I made it to the top out of White Bird Canyon which was super steep. Now it was time to go down the other side into Kooskia. It was the steepest, narrowest descent I had the whole journey. White knuckle would be an understatement. There were frequent switchbacks, and I was on the brakes the entire time. I didn't want to get up any speed because the turns were so sharp. I had to stop frequently to rest my hands, they were cramping from holding the bike back. At one point as I was stopped a car came up from below me. He rolled the window down and joked that it was a good thing I was going down! I'm not sure which was harder, pushing Crazy Horse up the steeps or keeping her under control on the descents!

I got into Kooskia and had a nice lunch, burger, fries, and a milkshake. There I noticed I had no cell service but thought little of it as I only had about 25 miles into Lowell, the stop for the night. I figured I'd have cell or at least wifi then. The rest of the ride was beautiful, flat, winding along the middle fork of the Clearwater River. I passed two young girls taking a swim, they waved and smiled as I passed by. I couldn't help but think about how lucky they were to grow up in such a place. They were somewhere around 11 or 12 years old, out on their own, no parents hovering around to make sure everything was okay. Just two kids hanging out on a summer day.

I got to the Wilderness Inn and Restaurant in Lowell by mid-afternoon. There were only 5 or 6 rooms, and I had to check in at the restaurant next door. The river looked so refreshing I asked if there was a good spot to swim nearby. It ran along the road just across the street. She said I could go in anywhere I could get down the bank. I quickly changed up and headed over, picking my way through bushes to get down to the water. I found a good spot and waded in, it wasn't deep, and the current moved swiftly. The water was just so crystal clear you could see every rock, pebble, and stone around you. As I sat there, I watched a young fawn get a drink on the far side. The water was chilly, so I eased my way in and sat against a large rock, letting the cool water soothe my tired legs. It was my 6th straight day in the saddle, and I had to get through tomorrow before I would take a day off.

Heading back to the room, I was getting a little concerned I still had no cell service. I needed to contact my niece, Laura, because we had to connect somewhere on the road into Missoula tomorrow. She had arranged for a place to stay so I wouldn't even know where to look for her.

Lowell may have been the smallest town I stayed in, though "town" is an overstatement. The sign said, "Welcome to Lowell, Idaho, population 24 23". I guess someone either moved or died.

There was a pay phone on the wall of a closed-up gas station next to the motel. I had some change with me and figured I could make a collect call to my sister to get a message to Laura. Who knows when the last time I tried to use a pay phone...decades ago??? It was dead, so I went over to the restaurant and asked if they had a pay phone. The girl just told me to use the phone by the register. I got a hold of my sister Jane and told her to text Laura and gave her the location to pick me up. I would have to hope she was there when I arrived! How did we ever survive without all our technology?!

After showering and relaxing, I went back to the restaurant to get dinner. It was the only food option available. I sat at the counter, and the girl said I had a phone message. Can't remember what it said but it didn't make sense. The young kid who took it couldn't remember what it was supposed to say. At least they had taken down the number for Laura's friend, Carly. I called Carly, whom I didn't know, and explained that I was Laura's aunt and I hoped they got the message about where to pick me up. Blind faith.

I ordered a burger and a beer. As I waited for my order the phone rang. The girl in charge answered and said it was for me. This was getting comical – I felt like I should own the place! It was Laura, and we hammered out the plan for the following day. I was excited to get to Montana and have a couple of days off!

From Jude's Jargon:

Time for a Little R & R

July 15, 2018

Believe I left off with my arrival in Grangeville, ID. Had a great dinner that night at a local spot. Met Casey, a Boise firefighter, and her Dad, they are natives of the Grangeville area. We had a fun conversation. Casey is the 3rd female to get on the Boise FD, and we compared experiences as I was the 4th female to get onto EPPD - though that was over 25 years ago. Guess Boise has some catching up to do! Her Dad had come to Idaho from Montana in the 70's as a "smoke-jumper," someone who jumps into fires from planes and helicopters to fight them. He liked the area and stayed. He cleared up the mysterious "time zone" issue! Back in the day, the mining companies in northern Idaho were determined to be in the same time zone as Spokane, hence the screwy set up throughout the state! I explained what I was doing and my route. They both said the route up through Lolo Pass was beautiful but to be careful as Route 12 was narrow and had a lot of truck traffic. I had already been advised of this and was nervous about it.

I took off from Grangeville the next morning headed for Lowell. I soon discovered that the name "Grangeville" was apt for the town. When I rode out of town, I encountered vast expanses of farmland, thousands of acres of hay and wheat fields. It differed totally from the arid, rocky ranch-land I'd been riding through for the past week. Most of the day I rode through the Nez Perce Indian Reservation. It is beautiful country. The story behind the Nez Perce, however, is not. They entered a treaty with the U.S. in 1855 which ceded 5.5 million acres of land to the U.S. for a nominal sum, and they were reduced to 7.5 million acres in the Northwest territory where no whites were supposed to settle. Gold was discovered on the land, and the U.S. refused to uphold the treaty. It led to war in 1877, and the Nez Perce ultimately surrendered. Those that surrendered were transported to Leavenworth and imprisoned. A tragic episode for our nation. Overall it was a peaceful ride through the fields and ultimately along the Clearwater River into Lowell.

Friday, I set out up Route 12 headed toward Lolo. I was apprehensive about the road and the traffic. I had

104

heard and seen the trucks going by the afternoon before and riding it didn't sound fun. I got going about 8:00, another beautiful, sunny day! Much to my surprise, it was an entirely peaceful and enjoyable ride along the Lochsa River. The traffic was light, and I only encountered a few trucks. I guess Friday's in the summer are slow around here too! At one point I saw a small outlet to my right which looked like river access, so I turned off. Sure enough, I got right down to the Lochsa. I snacked and drank some water and cooled off my feet in the water. Then I figured it was so nice and private I might as well go for a swim. Seeing that my bathing suit was not readily available, I might have taken a little skinny dip! (Don't tell anyone!) Seriously, there was not another soul around. Across the river was the Bitterroot Wilderness Area, a national park. It's territory that is largely untouched and in the same condition that Lewis & Clark found it in August 1805.

I finished the day near Lolo. Into Montana! I met up with my niece, Laura, and her friend Carly there. They had flown in the day before from Los Angeles. We got into the hotel and had dinner in Missoula, catching an awesome sunset at 9:45 p.m.! The next day we dropped Crazy Horse off at the shop for a new tire and a check-up and then headed north to Kerr Dam and Flathead Lake to kick around. We had a great, relaxing day! They had an early flight this morning back to L.A., but I took an extra day off and just knocked around Missoula for the afternoon. Two weeks in my body needed the rest, especially after 7 days in the saddle since my last day off. Tomorrow I head out to take on Montana, once I get through the "Great Divide" things should flatten out, and

I'll be able to pick up the mileage! Can't wait to see what tomorrow brings!

Other than the inconvenience of not having my cell phone available I didn't notice I was off the grid. It made for a quiet night that evening in Lowell with no internet, phone or email to deal with. I just read my book and went to sleep. So relaxing! I knew where I was and that I was safe so no big deal right? Three thousand miles away my friends weren't so relaxed. I guess they panicked a little when I dropped out of sight. They had grown used to watching my progress on the app and the occasional end of the day text about what I had seen and done that day. The texts flew around the neighborhood "have you heard from her" "nope, you?" and so on. I didn't have service most of the next day until I got to Missoula which didn't help them much.

My mental jury is still out about whether the technology is a good thing or bad. I can't imagine making the trip without it though. Another friend did it right after she graduated from college, before the days of laptops and cell phones. She spoke of creating their routes on the maps and being "the navigator." Only calling home at pay phones occasionally. It was different for her as she was with four other girls. I was alone and, most of the time knew that help was in the palm of my hand. I had a routine, when I got to my destination for the day, I'd go on line and book a room for the next night. It was so simple, just type "hotels in Missoula" into Google, and the list would come up. I could check price and availability without even picking up the phone. Boom—I'd book it and go to sleep knowing I was set for the next night. I'm not sure how I would have done it without those tools. Take the risk of getting into a town and hoping there was a hotel? And if there was, was there a room? I would have had to keep the camping gear with me.

THE COUNTRY CALLED MONTANA

As I prepared for the trip and told people my route took me through Montana, they always said they heard it was beautiful. Well, I can attest to it being beautiful. It is also HUGE! It became quite the joke back home in Rhode Island. Every day Beth's husband, Mike, would come home and ask Beth where I was. I guess he thought it was taking me a long time to get through Montana because his response after a few days was "when is she getting out of F)*&^%&ing Montana"! For a little perspective, consider that Montana is 121 times the size of Rhode Island. When I got to Missoula, I was about 850 miles in to the trip – I could have ridden the length of Rhode Island seventeen times at that point!

After spending the weekend in the second largest city, Missoula, I would cross the southern part of the state and go through some of the smallest towns imaginable and the most awesome display of wide-open space I'd ever seen. I was excited. So far, the journey had been amazing. Every day things got more beautiful and spectacular. I'd get on the bike each morning and ride into the unknown. What made it so cool was having no idea what was coming up around the next mountain. Would there be a ranch? Forest? River? What would the town be like? Would I meet interesting people at dinner?

A Day for Bugs, Among Other Things

July 17, 2018

So, the last two days I'd experienced Montana. I'm won't count the two days in Missoula because that was "city." I rode into Darby, population 730, yesterday from Missoula, 66 miles. It was uneventful, though enjoyable. It was uphill but so gradual you really couldn't feel the change in elevation. Fifty miles of it was a bike path alongside the road. Nice not to have to worry about traffic and trucks. I got into Darby at about 4:00 p.m. but had to hang around outside the motel for 45 minutes because the owner was off "doing errands" per the note on the door. I showered and walked down the street to the Sawmill to get some dinner and a beer or two. Met Lucas the bartender. He told me about his neighbor starting a fire which burned up most of the neighbor's property, fortunately not the house. I also chatted with Phil, a U.S. forest service worker. He was super nice. We talked about the route I was riding and what wildlife I might see along the way. I kept watch all day today but saw no moose, elk or bear! After dinner, walking back to the motel, I came across Brian and his horse, Molly. He had ridden 20 miles into town to grab a beer! It was interesting talking to these guys and everyone I've met. Particularly when I tell them what I'm doing. They get a far-away look and imagine what it would be like to just take off and go on an adventure!

Got up this morning ready to embark on the next leg of the journey. I knew it would be a fun day, I would be crossing the Continental Divide, heading to Jackson, Mt. about 76 miles. The first 35 miles would be tough, 4,000' climb to 7,250' at Chief Joseph Pass and the

Continental Divide. It was a better climb than those in Oregon and Idaho, not as steep and more gradual. However, it was still tough climbing for about 12 miles. I was into familiar territory, climb for a mile, stop, water, rest, shaky legs. I rode the whole thing though - success! I was averaging 5-6 mph. I passed by the 10,000 ft. Trapper's Peak.

Probably the worst part of the whole climb, other than the hill and the sweat, was the hummingbird-sized flies attacking me. One got a hold of my leg and drew blood! I swear those things were kamikazes! They buzzed around me for miles, and I couldn't go very fast as I was going uphill! I was swearing at them and trying to get them off me! People must have thought I was nuts - though we all know I am so no big deal! Finally got over the top and downhill! Headed to Wisdom for lunch about 20 miles away. I was getting tired; it had been a long morning climb. I had to stop at the Big Hole Battlefield. It was the site of the battle between the U.S. Army and the Nez Perce Tribe I wrote about the other day. It was neat, though sad. The territory was amazing. I had ridden out of the forest into the valley of huge, expansive prairie. The transformation was phenomenal. I continued into Wisdom and got some much-needed lunch, my blood sugar was getting low. It's amazing how in tune with my

113

body I'm getting on this ride. I can tell exactly when I need food and water and beer and sleep!

After lunch, I had only 18 miles to get into Jackson. It was about a 2,500' climb, but much like yesterday very gradual. I figured it to be a low-key ride. I may have been wrong about that. When I left Wisdom, it was lovely, warm and sunny though I could see rain showers up near the mountains I had just come through. I couldn't tell which way they were going, but it seemed they were heading west toward the mountains. I got 8 miles in and decided it was heading my way. I was racing the storm. I was Dorothy racing through Kansas trying to outrun the storm! I had stopped to take the photos and looked down and was covered in mosquitoes! Not more bugs! There was lightning and thunder in those clouds - better get going! As far as I can tell cows don't like thunder either, judging from the noise they were making! My relaxing ride became an adrenaline-infused sprint toward Jackson. I got beyond the storm to my west, merely getting rained on, when suddenly another popped up to the east! Damn! My legs were toast, and I was pushing it to 22 mph. I got by both with about two miles left to town. I was smoked!

As I pulled up to the Bunkhouse Hotel a man was out front covering up his motorcycle, "You must be the cyclist from Rhode Island," he said. "Yes, I am!" He told me the owner had stepped across the street but would be back shortly. Rick, the owner, came over a minute or two later. "It's Judy from Rhode Island!" Talk about a welcome. I took a quick shower and joined them at the next-door neighbor's front porch for cocktail hour. About a sixth of the town's population was there - six people - complete with pups! Been hanging out on the porch all evening. A perfect ending to yet another great day!

That night in Jackson was one of the best of the whole adventure, it was exactly the experience I was looking for when I set out. Being a life-long Rhode Islander, having only spent stints in high school and college living out of state, I was curious about how the rest of the country lived. It was one thing to talk to people about it and quite another to be in their environment and experience it.

The motorcyclist and I were the only guests at the Bunkhouse that night, and we hung around on the porch for the evening with Rick and a few other townsfolk. I wish I could remember the motorcyclist's name. He was so nice. He was retired, living in rural northern California and in the area to visit his son. At one point he asked Rick what the population of the town was. Rick paused a moment and said, "thirty-two" proceeding to count up one side of the street and down the other naming all the families. "Yup, thirty-two." Talk about small town!

Rick was an interesting character, he was about my age, 52, or perhaps a year or two younger. He was a retired town administrator from Washington state, though he did also mention being a police officer for 19 years too. He and his wife had bought the Bunkhouse as a retirement job and lived in an apartment off the back of the second floor. Their daughter was away at college.

He had every angle going in town, almost a de facto mayor. He had rehabbed the Bunkhouse, the only lodging in town, the post office was in the building, and he was the only purveyor of alcohol. It was funny. I went next door to the cantina, the only restaurant in town, to get something for dinner. When I asked what kind of beer they had, and the waitress said: "Oh, you have to get beer from Rick." I ordered my sandwich and walked back over to Rick's to get a beer. We talked for a few minutes then the owner of the cantina came over and told me my food was ready. You can't make this stuff up!

After dinner, we were hanging out on the porch in front of the Bunkhouse having a couple of beers. The conversation ranged widely from Rick's dispute with the county about the porch roof on the Bunkhouse, which he had built out to extend over the sidewalk, to the effect Amazon was having on local merchants, to guns to Rhode Island. They wanted to know how many Rhode Islands could fit into Beaver County – 4 – and Montana – 121. The gun discussion was interesting. You can see why Montanans are very pro-gun, for them guns are tools. They are ranchers and hunters. They may need to put down an injured cow or chase wolves or mountain lions away from their stock. Rick relayed a story about discovering that a mountain lion had been tracking him one day. When he returned from his hike, he could see the fresh paw prints that had followed behind him.

They were a little reticent to talk about it at first knowing I was from the northeast thus likely liberal. I told them I had no issue with guns and was familiar with handling them as I was a former cop. Rick immediately looked at me and said "I knew it! I could tell you were a cop." I said "look I get you guys like your guns; you respect them and use them properly. It's the shootings in the cities and assault weapons that bother most people." They were quick to point out there had been no mass shootings in Montana.

I could not imagine how a town that small could even survive. It wasn't exactly on the beaten path, the closest town with any population is Dillon with 4,000. They had to drive an hour and a half to get to a real grocery store. The local market had closed, they said, because they could order anything on line, have it in two days and pay less. Doesn't take a rocket scientist to figure that one out. I wish I had asked them about healthcare. I'm sure access to doctors was as limited as access to supermarkets. Knowing general practitioners are scarce, even in such places as Providence, it must be doubly hard to get them to these thinly populated areas.

After a couple of hours of laughs and good conversation, it was time to get some sleep. Besides, it was getting downright cold! Jackson was at 6,500 feet, so the air was thin and when the sun set the temperature plummeted. After reaching a high in the low 90's that day, it would dip into the 40's overnight. Brrr. I would be off to Dillon in the morning.

Revenge of the Human!

July 19, 2018

The last few days have been somewhat uneventful. Yesterday rode from Jackson to Dillon about 47 miles. Frankly, I was beaten up from the day before, crossing the Divide and racing thunderstorms did a number on me. It was hard to leave my new friend, Abby, in Jackson. Two passes yesterday, Big Hole Pass 7,400 ft and Badger Pass 6,600, they weren't terrible, but my legs were spent so probably a little harder than on a fresh day. Although the last 15 miles into Dillon was all downhill, I got up to 30-35 mph. Getting into town around 2:00 p.m. I had some time to relax and watch TV, maybe a little nap too.

I found what looked to be one of the better places in town and headed over for dinner. As you can tell by previous posts, I sit at the bar so I can meet new people and chat. I got to Mac's Bar & Grill and found a seat at the bar. As I sat down, I could tell they were talking about cycling and eating. The guy a couple of seats over had a huge plate of ribs, and they were talking about burning calories riding. He was obviously a rider. Another gentleman was an engineer from Big Fork

121

passing through on business, and another was a recent transplant from Texas, he liked to mountain bike.

We had a nice conversation about Montana and the geography. The engineer and his wife had moved out here a few years ago from Cincinnati and were loving it. Their sons were all west coast based, so it was a no-brainer. The guy from Texas said he was having a tough time riding with the change in altitude but was slowly getting used to it. He got up to leave and told the bartender he was taking care of me and the other rider. I thought he was just buying us a drink, but no, he was picking up out dinners! He thought what we were doing was so cool he wanted to do something for us. Yet another random act of kindness.

The other rider was Ted, at teacher at the Belmont Hill School outside Boston. He was riding from Jasper, Alberta to Boulder, Co. Turns out he had done quite a few tours in his day. He said when he started up in Canada, he got snowed on. I'll stick with the hot it's more enjoyable! We all went our separate ways for the night.

This morning I caught up with Ted on the road just outside of Dillon. We were going in the same direction. He was the first person I'd seen heading east! We road together for about 25 miles to Two Bridges. It was a great, flat ride and we were averaging over 15 mph. There wasn't too much traffic so we could converse easily. He had followed the same route I had from Missoula and had probably only been a few hours behind me. We compared notes on crossing the Divide at Chief Joseph Pass and agreed it was difficult. I said the worst part may have been the flies. He said they were brutal, but he had killed a couple. I sincerely hope he got the one that drew blood on my leg!!! Revenge!

We got to Twin Bridges and stopped to get a drink and sit in the air-conditioned market for a few minutes. We were headed opposite ways out of town, so our ride together was short lived but pleasant. He was heading down toward Yellowstone and Wyoming while I'm going east to Bozeman. He has a lot more climbing to do. Thankfully, I have one gentle climb over Bozeman Pass, and I'll be onto the Plains! The mountains were beautiful, as were the valleys. However, I came to discover that as beautiful as the valleys were, there is always a pass to go over to get out! The price of admission. Spending tonight in Whitehall, Mt. then on to Bozeman tomorrow. It will be another flat and short ride. I'll likely spend the day there Saturday too and then ramp up the miles on Sunday. I'll finally be turning eastward. I'm just over 1,000 miles in but have been meandering around in the mountains in various directions trying to get through them. I can only imagine how Lewis & Clark felt hauling all their goods with canoes and only making 20-30 miles on a good day. It has been fun though. I'm reading the book "Undaunted Courage" about Lewis & Clark's expedition, parts have coincided with my location on the trail. The terrain is unchanged but for the roads.

Well - off until next time! Let's hope the wind is with me on the Plains!

Road to Nowhere
July 21, 2018
I'm feelin' okay this mornin'
And you know

We're on the road to paradise
Here we go, here we go
We're on a ride to nowhere
Come on inside
Takin' that ride to nowhere
We'll take that ride
(Talking Heads, Road to Nowhere, 1985)

Left Whitehall, Mt. yesterday morning setting out for Bozeman. It would be a 68-mile trek over rolling hills. The first 20 miles were gorgeous! The great thing about being near the interstate is that traffic is cut down immensely. I rode along the Jefferson River through winding roads surrounded by steep hills. I was the only person out there, just me and the cows. Every field I go by they watch me. Their eyes follow me, and their heads turn with me as I go by. I'm sure they all are wondering what these crazy people on bikes are doing!

Breakfast had been a little lean at the Rodeway Inn. My choice of cereal was Frosted Flakes, Corn Pops, Fruit Loops or Apple Jacks. I went for the Apple Jacks - just for you Dairsie! Add a blueberry bagel (who knew they made those!), and it was a breakfast of champions! I stopped in Three Forks about 10:30 for something a little more substantial. Three Forks is a nice little town and was a stop for the Lewis & Clark Expedition Westward in 1805. Three rivers converge there, and Capt. Lewis named them the Jefferson, for President Jefferson; the Madison for Secretary of State James Madison; and the Gallatin, for Secretary of the Treasury Albert Gallatin. Had a great omelet at the local diner and moved on toward Bozeman.

I headed out of town on a road that runs parallel to I-90. It was narrow with no shoulder. The traffic wasn't too bad but, after a few miles, I spotted a bike path between my road and the interstate. I hopped on hoping that I would have an experience like a few days ago when I went for 50+ miles on a path. It went along great for a couple of miles when suddenly there was a stop sign and the pavement just ended. It looked like kind of a dirt path from there on so I kept going, only to discover that it was loose gravel and I would not make it far without having the bike skid out from beneath me. I stopped and considered my options. I could go back - nonstarter - I refuse to go backwards. I could go over to the road through tall grass and climb out of the 4' ditch back onto the road. I chose plan B. I wheeled Crazy Horse into the ditch and the grass, watching out for any snakes that may have been lurking. Got to the side of the road and had to take all my gear off the bike to get out of the ditch. I must have been a sight, cursing and hurling my heavy bags onto the road! I should have taken a picture of the stop sign on the path to nowhere, it was funny. However, I was staying true to my rule - no going backwards! Someone at Montana DOT got a kick out of putting the sign there I'm sure.

Got into Bozeman about 3:00 p.m. I had seen a billboard on the interstate sponsored by the Boys & Girls Club, and I looked up the local club. Google got me there in no time. At first, I had a difficult time finding it on the road because it looks like a private house. When I got close, I found the small sign for the club. It was in a house! It was so quiet I wondered if anyone was there, but the door was unlocked, so I walked in. A young staff member met me as I came in and recognized the Club logo on my shirt. Told her what I was doing, and I was stopping in to say hi. She introduced me to the Director, Jeanne. They offered me some water, and we chatted for a few minutes. Jeanne gave me a brief history of the club. They had recently moved to this location, a model home for the nearby development. It was nice, they had turned all the rooms into separate activity areas. The nicest home some of these kids may ever see. Jeanne's husband came in, he volunteers, and gave me the full tour. They have a barn adjacent to the house which he is remodeling to use for more activities. They are also next to a 100-acre natural public park which they have access to. The kids were finishing their water week program and having water balloon fights in the yard. It all seemed idyllic, but these kids face similar issues to those our kids see in Providence. Poor, single-parent families or drug problems, the drug of choice is methamphetamine, and many parents struggle with addiction.

Different states, same mission for the Boys & Girls Club - help these kids succeed! Jeanne mentioned that they had one of their top kids earn a scholarship to Brown University - she was rightly very proud. As I write this, I'm certain that my ride has generated over $50,000 in donations for the Providence Clubs. Thank you to those of you who have contributed! If you would like to help support the cause, you can donate through the following link: *https://bgcprov.org/judy-davis-cross-country-bike-ride/*

While I'm having a blast doing the ride - I also keep in mind that there is a greater purpose! Thanks, Judy

I spent a nice day off in Bozeman, a place I'd like to return to someday. They were having their summer sale days, a huge sidewalk sale on the main drag. I wandered around and checked out the shops. It was a good, lazy day. I was now almost three weeks into the trip and had covered 1,100 miles. I still had 2,700 miles to go and only 5 weeks to do it in to make it back by Labor Day. This meant I would have to ramp up the miles. Fortunately, I was about to leave the Rockies behind and head for flatter ground. It was like a never-ending summer. Remember when you were a kid, and you got out of school in the spring? It felt like forever before you went back in September? That's exactly how I felt. Though it was not as carefree as a summer of my youth, I had a lot of work in front of me. And I still had almost 400 miles still to go in f^#&*#@g Montana!

From Jude's Jargon:

Last Pass!!!

July 22, 2018

Finally, the last significant climb for a long time is over and done with! Left Bozeman at about 7:30 a.m. I wanted to get an early start because I knew I would put in a few miles today. Another good reason to start early is the temperature, when I left it was around 55 degrees. The air is so dry, and with the elevation, it cools down quickly at night. Today was a perfect riding day. When I arrived in Columbus, MT at 4:00 p.m. it was only 75.

There were a few "firsts" today too. My route would take me onto Interstate 90 for the first time. Yes, it's legal to ride a bike on the interstate in Montana. I got on a few miles outside of Bozeman for a 6-mile stretch. The first thing you need to look out for are the cattle-guards that are on the road and on the ramps. They are huge metal grates that span the entire lane. The gaps are

130

wide, so you must make sure you are perpendicular as you cross. I'm assuming the cattle won't walk over them, so it keeps them off the highway. The first stretch was okay, but the shoulders weren't quite as wide as I'd expected, they were there, nonetheless, so I wouldn't be in the travel lane. This was the initial part of the climb up Bozeman Pass, elevation 5,700'. I was only going 9-10 mph. Not a bad climb. I got off and had about three more miles before I hit the pass. Once over the top, I had a beautiful 5-7 mile downhill. I experienced a huge relief getting over that. My ride from here to the Berkshires is relatively flat, rolling hills, but no real elevation. I'm already down to about 3,600' and tomorrow it will be about 2,700'. I did a couple more stretches on I-90, and it was just fine with shoulders 8-10' wide. It beat going up Route 12 in Idaho with no shoulders and having eighteen wheeler's and logging trucks buzz past you at 60 mph!

After the pass the ride was innocuous. The view was consistent mountains on both sides and mostly along the Yellowstone River. I stopped for lunch in Big Timber, MT, 60 miles into the day. After lunch, it was on to Columbus. On the way into town, I did finally see a couple of elk. They crossed the road in front of me by about 100 yards. They got into the brush quickly, so I couldn't get a photo. The day ended with another fist, I

131

cracked the 100-mile per day barrier, 102 to be exact. With the terrain being flat I'm hoping to get in 80-100 per day, this pace should get me home before Labor Day. I'm excited for the change of scenery. The mountains were beautiful, but I will not miss riding up or down them!

On another note, my college friends will appreciate this one - I found the western annex of the Cedar Inn! I spent the day off yesterday walking around Bozeman. They were having their "Crazy Days," so all the stores on the main drag were having Crazy Day sales. I spent the afternoon window shopping and checking things out. Bozeman is a nice town, so I'm glad I poked around. I went back to the hotel around four to relax and decide where to eat dinner. The hotel was about 3/4 of a mile outside the retail/restaurant district where I spent the afternoon, and I didn't want to walk back up there, especially as I knew I had a long day today. I went on Google Maps and found the Haufbrau House literally on the side street next to my hotel. It had good ratings so why not???

I walked in and immediately felt like I was walking right into the Cedar. Hard to explain but it just had that feel. Here are a few pics, those of you who are familiar should see the resemblance!

Everything was just so similar it was eerie. The same dilapidated building, faux leather booths, stuff hanging on the walls dating back 30+ years, even the food, though no wings, it was all there. My burger even came out in one of those plastic baskets with the red and white checked paper liner! The bartender was super nice even gave me a drink chip, yet another similarity, when I told him about my ride. The Montana State kids hang out there when school's in session. It was a trip down memory lane.

Sorry to all who have never been to the Cedar, just a little digression. However, if you're ever in Geneva, NY, check it out. Not fine dining but that's more than made up for with character!

This discussion of food has made me hungry! Off to find tonight's local joint, another big day tomorrow!

Bozeman to Columbus was my first ever 100-mile plus ride. After taking a day off, it didn't seem too bad. I checked into the Riverside Cabins for the evening and, as usual, washed off the stress of the day in the shower. It was a great little spot right across the road from the Yellowstone River. I'd spent most of the day riding along the river which made for little elevation change over the 100 miles, thankfully. The Riverside Cabin was about the fourth "cabin" I'd stayed in so far on the trip. They are a great option. Much homier than a typical hotel room and very quaint. Most had pine paneled walls, quilts on the beds and windows that opened for fresh air! They also had great wifi. Most were inexpensive, under a $100 per night, with one in North Dakota at $45.00! What a bargain!

After cleaning up, I walked down the street to find dinner. Having seen chicken fried steak on the menu at almost every stop along the way, I figured it was time to go out on a limb and try it. I had no idea what to expect. Would it be like a NY strip battered and fried or what?

Come to find out, chicken fried steak is ground beef battered and fried then smothered with gravy. I didn't find it that exceptional. My mistake was I only tried it that one time, so I had nothing to compare it too. Maybe that was bad chicken fried steak? Who knows?? On my way back to the cabin I stopped at the Thirsty Turtle Saloon to check it out. As it was a Sunday night, there were only a couple of people there. The lack of people was made up for by the number of dead animals hanging on the walls! There were all kinds of species, elk, deer, bear, moose, mountain lions. It was crazy but interesting. After my beer with the wild things, I headed back to get some rest before another big day.

From Jude's Jargon:

What A Difference A Day Makes!

July 24, 2018

Not going to sugarcoat this, Monday was by far the worst day of the ride. It sucked! I was traveling from Columbus, MT to Custer, MT, about 98 miles and I had to go through Billings. The morning wasn't too bad, though I knew I'd be facing headwinds all day. The wind picked up as I approached Billings, it wasn't a bother then as traversing the city slowed me down. Billings is the largest city in Montana, population 110,000, it was like driving down Rte. 2 in Warwick. Lots of traffic over many lanes. At one point I missed a turn, and it cost me about four extra miles, ugh. Grabbed a bite to eat there then got going again as I still had 50 miles to cover.

It was 18-20 miles to the next town, Worden, I figured I'd stop there and get a snack - preferably a milk shake! I was headed due east, and the wind was coming from due east. It was only 5-8 mph, which doesn't seem like much, but it is relentless. I made it to Worden and got my shake but still had 32 miles to go and knew it would be no fun. I started up and headed right back into the wind. The terrain wasn't bad, flat with little to no traffic. I was averaging 10-12 mph but getting beaten up the whole way. It was demoralizing. With no wind or a slight tail wind, I'd be doing 14-16mph. Over 50-60 miles that makes a huge difference in time in the saddle. I was stopping every 5 miles or so to get some water and rest for a minute or two. Mile markers become important. My legs didn't feel too bad even after 100+ the day before. Your whole body wears out at that point because you continue to get beat down by the wind.

To make matters worse, I must have been allergic to something, so my nose was constantly running. Told you there wouldn't be any sugarcoating! I was working my tail off over those last 30 miles, sweat/salt stained, snot nosed with grease streaks on my leg - so attractive! Well, I did finish 9.5 hours after beginning with 8.75 of those in the saddle - thoroughly mentally and physically exhausted.

I got into my destination, Custer, population 159, at 6 p.m. I was staying at the Junction City Saloon which has three rooms, not numbered but colored, the green room was mine. I had to check in at the bar. One of those places when the door opens everything stops and everyone looks to see who has arrived. I ordered a pizza, which they promptly took out of the freezer and baked for me, got a couple of beers and retired to the "green room." Thankfully they had wifi so I could watch the Sox game!

That day was in the top five worst of the trip, second, only topped by the next to last day of the journey from Albany to Springfield. It was hot and windy, but the worst part was navigating Billings. I had become so used to the "open road," and this was the first city I had encountered since Eugene. I never got into the center of the city, relegated to the outskirts with the typical urban sprawl. It could have been any state as I passed by the chain restaurants and stores, Red Lobster, Olive Garden, Target, Wal-Mart. You get the idea. You have to ride on the sidewalk because the traffic is so heavy. That's not terrible because no one is walking on the sidewalk and they're new, so wide. It just slowed me down.

Billings was also the site of my only close encounter with a motor vehicle, thankfully only a slow speed crash! I didn't write about it in the blog because it was still early in the trip and I didn't want anyone at home to get upset. It was around noon; I was hungry having ridden 50 miles. First, I needed to find a place to pick up supplies like shampoo, etc. Finding that stuff in the small towns was hard. I stopped at an intersection and would go straight across when the light changed. It was a big intersection, four lanes of traffic each way. The light changed in my favor, and I started across slowly. Suddenly a pick-up truck fender came into me from the left. It all happened in slow motion. I realized the truck was turning in front of me and we would collide. I veered to my right, but I was going so slowly that I "cow-tipped" and fell over onto the side walk. Cow tipping is when you're going so slow that you just fall over, mainly because you're clipped in to your pedals and just can't get your feet out quick enough. A helpless feeling!

I wasn't hurt, just pissed off. I got up and looked at the guy in the truck. He didn't get out, or anything just pointed at the sign that said right turn.

"Really???" I was so mad. He couldn't wait the 2, count them 2, seconds it would have taken for me to pass in front of him??? Other people were more caring and asked if I was okay, equally miffed at the guy. I was fine. It just added to what became a very bad day. It was the closest I came to being hit by a car the entire trip, so all in all not bad.

I was just happy that I could retire to my "green room" for the night and watch the Red Sox. I had another big day on the horizon the next day, 97 miles to Miles City.

From Jude's Jargon:

Today started much better, the forecast wind was WNW, perfect! It would be at my back! The first 50 miles were peaceful. I was on a back road with no traffic. The only thing that came to mind to compare it to is playing golf on a summer evening when you're the only person on the course, the colors are vibrant, the greenest green you'll ever see as the sun goes down and the shadows grow long. This was the same only magnified by a thousand! I crossed over the Yellowstone River which was beautiful. Then I got into ranch country and met new friends, pictured. This is what the sign "open range" means. These gals were just hanging out by the side of the road. I stopped about 25 yards away to get the photo. They were fully engaged with me, watching my every move. As I was getting things back together, the largest cow moved out into the road. Uh oh, some of these cows looked young, so maybe that was mamma? I got going slowly, and Mamma immediately took off for the other side of the road. The rest of them followed her. All I could think of was the potential headline in the next day's paper "Cyclist Trampled by Cattle." Though it likely wouldn't have been in the next day's paper as I'm not certain a car even went down the road that day!

While that day was much better than the previous, it was still almost a hundred miles in 90-degree heat. I remember getting into the outskirts of Miles City and stopping at the nearest gas station to get a cold drink. I sat on the curb outside the door and gulped down sixty-four ounces of icy cold Gator Aid. My legs were jelly, and I had another 80 miles to get to Glendive the next day. I had done almost three hundred miles over three days. I didn't wrap my head around it then, though it almost makes me cry thinking about it as I write this four months later. I was so spent my body and mind were limp. I just concentrated on getting up the next day and doing it again. Had I put any thought into it at that moment I would have cried.

I got myself up the next morning and set out for Glendive, my last stop in Montana. It felt good to be getting closer to the eastern border of the state. It seemed I'd been in Montana forever. I continued to follow the Yellowstone River as I had since leaving Bozeman the previous Sunday. It's a beautiful river and is the longest free-flowing river in the contiguous United States, dams haven't been built along it to create lakes. I hit the wall along the way to Glendive and knew that I would need to take the next day off. My body had had enough.

There's little going on in Glendive, a city of about 5,000 people, so I didn't do a lot on my day off. My hotel was on the outskirts, so there was little around within walking distance. I had to check out the dinosaur museum across the street. They had recovered many fossils in the area, which made sense once I thought about the terrain I'd been riding through. The museum's theory on dinosaur's and the prehistoric period is unique. The basic premise is that the dinosaurs were part of God's creation and there was no prehistoric period. Fossils of sea creatures found thousands of miles from the ocean were explained by the flood of Genesis. It was rather a different take on things, and I will leave it to the geologists, archeologists, and theologists to debate. One thing was for sure though, I was no longer in Rhode Island!

From Jude's Jargon:

Montana Musings

July 26, 2018

Yesterday's ride from Miles City to Glendive, MT was uneventful 78 miles. My good friend named Headwind joined me on the last 20 miles. I was spent having done close to 400 miles in 4 days, so my body and Crazy Horse talked me into a day off today. I did see some wildlife yesterday, pronghorns, more deer, and cattle. A bald eagle flew along with me for a few minutes. I asked if she was related to the Rumford bald eagles, but she didn't answer.

Since there's not much to do in Glendive, aside from visiting the dinosaur museum, I'm hanging around the hotel relaxing and doing laundry. It has given me time to reflect on some random thoughts that have crossed my mind about Montana.

Montana is HUGE! To give some perspective - it's 147,040 sq. miles - you can fit 121 RI's into it or two New England's!

RI has about a 10,000-person population edge - 1,060,000 to 1,050,000

Montanan's also like their vanity plates

Seems like everyone owns an RV that resembles a Rolling Stones Tour Bus and tows their car and sometimes car and boat behind it.

Prairie dogs are just squirrels that live in holes.

There must be some kind of state ban on Heineken. (Apparently, no Kane's allowed.)

Out here when a street is named "Broadway," it's Broadway Ave. or Broadway St. - just weird!

I really want to know where the Continental Divide of the "soda" versus "pop" classification is. More than one store clerk thinks I'm an alien.

Road signs were invented for target practice.

Ranchers have replaced their horses with vehicles which are a cross between golf carts and dune buggies.

Cows are people too.

There are exits off the interstate that serve one ranch - imagine your own driveway exit off I-95.

144

Golf courses are generally located on "Golf Way" and cemeteries on "Cemetery St."

Supermarkets are few and far between.

Well, I think I'll head over and check out the dinosaur museum. Into North Dakota and yet another time zone tomorrow. Farewell Montana.

ON TO THE BADLANDS!

I got up refreshed my last morning in Montana. Had my usual breakfast, several bowls of cereal and a bagel along with coffee and juice, packed up Crazy Horse and set off for North Dakota. I barely made it out of the parking lot before I noticed something was wrong. Crazy Horse didn't feel right. I turned back to the hotel and checked her out. I discovered the problem; my rear tire was close to flat. "Oh man!" I thought to myself. "Why couldn't I have discovered this yesterday??" It was time for an executive decision. Should I unload everything and change out the tube and maybe the tire too, or, pump it up and see how far I got? The treads were looking flat, so I probably did need the new tire, but did I want to take the time to change everything right then?? What made the decision even harder, or easier, was that I was trying to get to Dickinson, ND, a 100-mile trek.

I chose plan B, pump up the tire and see how far I got. It was the easy way out and likely stupid, but the thought of unloading everything and changing out the tire was unappealing. It made the day stressful. I worried the tire would go flat at any moment and I would end up changing it at the side of the road anyway. The first leg didn't help. I had 36 miles to go to get to the next town, Beach, ND, 20 miles of it on Interstate 94.

Things went well, the tire held up okay. It was overcast, not too hot, which was nice. As I approached the North Dakota border, there were two cyclists ahead of me on the Interstate. I figured they would stop at the sign for a picture as I planned to do. After all, it was an occasion to celebrate, I would finally be out of F*&^$ing Montana! They were there as expected, and it worked out well because we could take each other's photos without having to struggle to get the sign in with a selfie. We chatted for a few minutes. They were a young couple in their mid to late 20's. She had just finished her graduate work in Seattle, and they were riding home to the D.C. area. They had an interesting theory about riding on the Interstate which I reflected on in Jude's Jargon.

From Jude's Jargon:

Everyday It's Something July 29, 2018

I've been a little remiss over the last few days about writing. Frankly, I've been too tired. After a needed but uneventful day in Glendive, MT (though I did check out the dinosaur museum) I headed out Friday morning for Dickinson, N. Dakota. I knew it would be a long day, 100 miles to cover, but I didn't expect to be on the road for 11 hours! I should have known when I got on Crazy Horse and the rear tire was low. Decision time - change it or pump it up and see what happens. I chose option B and kept my fingers crossed. The first 36 miles to Beach, ND combined I-94 and "frontage road." As I've said the interstate isn't too bad to ride, the shoulders are wide and the surfaces good, but the frontage roads are even better. For the most part, it's been Old Highway 10, though it's named various things in various places. These roads parallel the interstate and have essentially no traffic. I was on the interstate as I approached the state line. Unbelievable, I never thought I'd get through Montana! It took two weeks to wind my way up down and around! There were a couple of cyclists ahead of me and, as I assumed, they stopped at the sign. Nice young couple, we chatted and took photos for each other. They were headed from Seattle to Maryland. As we discussed the roads and routes, they said they preferred to stay on the interstate. Whaat?? Youth is wasted on the young! I told them the frontage roads were awesome, so much to see, beautiful scenery, towns, people. The interstate isn't a bad ride, but the cars and trucks are still going past you at 80-90 mph (speed limit is 80). I would just be so tense the whole way. Oh well, to each his own.

148

I stopped in Beach for lunch, only 36 miles into a 100-mile ride. I already felt behind. I checked the tire and pumped it up again. It would need some attention at some point that day. I continued Old Highway 10 and rode through some light rain showers, only the second time in a month of riding I'd seen any rain. Got into Medora, ND and came across the entrance of The Theodore Roosevelt National Park. Glad I went through there, he's one of my favorite presidents. I do think he would be disappointed to see the town today though. It's quaint enough but was crawling with tourists, most coming into town in the own personal tour buses!

Fortunately for me, there was a great little bike shop into town, Dakota Cyclery, owned by a great couple who've been in the bike business for 40 years. They squared me away with a new tire and tube, the one I got in Missoula just wasn't holding up. This one is one of the best out there - hopefully it will see me home. Left the shop around 4:00 p.m. still with 30 miles to go, ugh. Didn't get to Dickinson until 6:45, a long day. Was more uphill than I anticipated, and the tire issue didn't help.

Had a good night in Dickinson and set off yesterday for Mandan, another long one 97 miles. I was hoping that it would be uneventful. Most of it was rolling hills, some climbing but not too bad. The wind was good

149

too. The only thing that worried me was a 10 mile stretch of gravel road about 60 miles into the day. The alternative to gravel was going on the interstate through a section where the entire shoulder was chatter strip. That sounded awful so gravel it was. Crazy Horse handled it beautifully, she is, after all, a "gravel bike." It was okay for the first few miles but got old fast. More rolling hills made more difficult due to the terrain. The whole stretch slowed me down. It's not so hard on the legs but is on hands, arms, shoulders and upper back. It's very tense trying to keep a loaded bike from sliding out from under you! At one point a guy came by in a car. He said he didn't see many bikes on that road. "Well," I said, "the alternative is rumble strip on the highway." He agreed it was a toss-up! I don't know which is worse, but I'm not going back to find out! Another long day! None of the cafes were open in the towns I passed through so no good lunch. I was relegated to water and trail mix - not enough! Did almost an entire pizza for dinner and was still hungry when I woke up this morning!

Today would be shorter, 78 miles, and I hoped that it would be uneventful. No tire problems, no route problems, and no weather problems. I almost got that! First 50 miles were nice! Crossed the Missouri River in Bismarck and went through rolling hills until I got to

150

Hazelton. So far so good! The only thing open in town was a gas station/convenience store/sandwich shop. Well, you can imagine that my cheese-steak sandwich was less than ideal; however, it was better than trail mix! Chatted with the clerk while she had a cigarette break outside, she lives in Napoleon, the town I'm staying in tonight. She was nice. Told me I was the 3rd or 4th lone female to come cycling through. She'd just talked to her Dad in Napoleon, and it was raining there. We looked in that direction, and it appeared so. The plains are so vast you can see around you for miles and see the rain cells where ever they are. It was a very scenic ride - crops all around for miles and miles - sunflowers, wheat, and corn. I set out for Napoleon, 26 miles away. It did appear that I would be riding right into the rain and of course, Mr. Headwind showed up. Really??? I was so close to getting away with a benign day! The headwind was strong, I assume from the rain ahead, probably close to 10 mph. Combined with the rolling hills it slowed me down to 8-10 mph. My short leg would take a while. The rain stayed south of me but came close. As I got by it, the wind switched to southerly and got a little stronger. I was hanging onto the bike and leaning into it to the right to stay toward the side of the road. Hoped that it would come all the way around to westerly! No such luck but the further I got beyond the rain it got weaker. Then my last six miles were downhill - thankfully! When this stuff comes up it's so mentally exhausting - gravel, wind, hills - they just keep beating on you.

Well, tomorrow is another day, though a long one, 105 miles. However, according to my maps, I should be out of the hills early on and into the flats! The weather forecast has the wind coming out of the west - finally!! Let's hope I can get through it without something else coming up!!! Tuesday will be a short day and should have a day and a half in Fargo to kick around and rest!

Napoleon, ND is a quaint little town of about 750 people. It sits on McKenna Lake and is dominated by a tremendous grain elevator. I was staying in another cute little cabin. It was nice to open the window and get some fresh air while I slept. It got cold that night, down into the high forties. I walked through town to find the place the store clerk at lunch had recommended. It was a nice little restaurant/bar, quiet on that Sunday night. The whole town was quiet, prototypical mid-west. The houses were modest clapboard designs, there was an Elks Club, Town Hall, courthouse and a school. I later discovered that a friend in Rhode Island went to school in the town from kindergarten through high school. It is a small world!

The next day's ride was interesting, not for its scenery, as wonderful as usual, but for the route. Being from the east, I'm used to winding roads and city streets that turn this way and that. New England streets are so old, and there was not a lot of planning. As the population grew and expanded towns and cities evolved, which made for labyrinths of city streets. The differences in places like North Dakota are several. First, there's little population, so the distances between towns are great, and, they were built later with more planning. This made for an orderly grid pattern.

I set out from Napoleon to Enderlin, ND that day. I headed east on Rte. 34 for about 20 miles through wide-open farm country. It was dead straight without as much as a curve in the road. From there I took a left onto Rte. 30 for another straight 10 miles until I got to Rte. 46 and took a right to continue eastward. That was the last turn I would make for the day, and I still had over 80 miles to ride. Think about that for a minute, I rode 80 miles dead straight without making one turn. The only curve in the road came when I crossed the James River, and that wasn't even much of a curve. Talk about monotonous!

It was also a thinly populated stretch. My maps had me prepared for "limited services" so I had plenty of water and snacks with me. I had a pleasant surprise when I got to the junction of Rte. 281 as there was a new gas station/café not reflected on my map. It was a welcome sight as I was hot and tired. Inside I got a Coke and some ice cream. There were a few tables, so I could sit and relax in the air conditioning for a few minutes before making the final push to Enderlin 40 miles later.

A gentleman in his 80's came in and ordered a coffee. It was apparent this was his daily routine given his conversation with the clerk. He sat down at the next table, and we struck up a conversation. He had seen my bike outside and asked where I was headed. I explained the trip, and he thought it was great. We talked about trucks. He was sympathetic, having spent his life in the immediate area. There wasn't much of a shoulder and given the straight, flat terrain they had been flying by me all day. It gets nerve racking after a while, especially when they're coming from both directions, there wasn't room for two 18-wheelers and me on the road. My nerves were raw by the finish. I enjoyed the conversation. It felt good to add a little spice to the man's day. He had an opportunity to share my adventure and reminisce about days gone by.

I bid him goodbye and headed out for Enderlin. Turns out I was lucky that day. When I pulled up to the hotel, a gentleman in the parking lot said, "you'd better hurry up and check in, there's only one room left."

Wow, I thought. I hadn't booked a room in advance thinking there were two motels in the town, and it was a Monday night. I soon discovered that there was only one room left. I snapped it up and headed for a shower! Time for dinner and a good night's rest before heading on to Fargo in the morning for my last stop in North Dakota.

Move Over Curt Schilling, There's a New Bloody Sock In Town

July 30, 2018

Well, the worst moment of my day today happened before 8:00 a.m. Golfers in the crowd will relate. You're getting ready for your round, you may chip a little, putt a little, hit a few balls. You're next on the tee, and your friends are waiting, you gather up your clubs while you're talking to them and going from the putting green to the tee. As you walk to the tee your wedge slips and whacks your ankle, ouch! I can feel you all cringing right now - there's no pain quite like banging your ankle bone with an iron except slamming your bike pedal into it! I did that outside the coffee shop this morning and boy did it hurt! Who knew cycling was a contact sport! But as I mentioned it was the worst part of my day. My ride was kind of like that round of golf where you just go along, and things work out. You do nothing spectacular, but at the end of the day, you have a great score. Drive - fairway - green - two putts - par. Ho hum.

I started from Napoleon around 8:00 a.m., the conditions were perfect, cool, no wind, not a cloud in the sky! I knew it would be a long day as, according to my maps, there were limited services for a 78-mile stretch. I wanted to get to Enderlin so I would have a short 50-mile hop into Fargo tomorrow. For most of the morning, I had no traffic, maybe 4-5 cars went by me over several hours. So just me, the cows and acres and acres of crops all around. I had gently rolling hills for about 40 miles then it got flat - really flat. I could average 16-18 mph. What wind there was was at my back - finally! It was incredibly peaceful.

I realized as I rode why things move a little slower out here and people are so relaxed. There's just so much space - you never feel crowded. Think about it, most of you reading this live on the east coast and the population is dense. Your neighbors are close, you deal with traffic every day, you stand in line at stores to check out, you have to worry about making reservations at a good restaurant, the newly released movie may be sold out, and on and on and on. We are just constantly crowded. In my humble opinion, it adds a certain level of stress to our everyday lives. Trust me I have stress on this journey, but the abundance of space is relaxing. That's my deep thought of the day if you were wondering what I think about over all those miles!

That was my day. I made it to Enderlin, a 112-mile trek - I know I said 105 last night. I do words, people, words! Not math - as many of you know! There was one annoyance along the way, and my cycling pals will relate. You know those seams that run across roads? Often, they are tarred over to fill them in, but they're like little trenches - you know the ones. Well, they get REALLY annoying when you go over them forty-seven thousand times a day! I had a good 30-40 miles of one every 10-15 yards. Ka-thump, ka-thump, ka-thump, ka-thump. I think some of my teeth are loose! Poor Crazy Horse.

Some of you may be wondering what I'm doing for accommodations each night. For the most part, it's motels. It's hard enough to be outside working your tail off all day riding to think about camping. A lot of the kids I've met along the way are camping most of the time. Frankly, I enjoy my shower and bed every night! Probably 3 or 4 times I've been in small towns and found there are cabins available. I have to say they're quite nice. The photo is of the one I stayed in last night - The Broken Bell Inn in Napoleon, ND. I called in the morning to make the reservation. The owner took my info and said I'd be in Cabin 3; the key and receipt would be in there upon my arrival. Sure enough, when I pulled in around 4, it was all there ready to go. No check in needed, I never saw the owner. I have to say the best thing was opening the windows and sleeping in the fresh air! It got cool last night, forty-seven when I awoke, perfect sleeping weather. Beats motel air conditioning!

That's my tale for the day. Time to find some dinner!

HALFWAY!

It was August 2nd when I set out for Fargo from Enderlin, the halfway point in the journey. I figured I should be able to make it home by Labor Day. I had upped the pace since leaving Bozeman. In those 8 days, I got in over 760 miles, and that was only 7 days of riding as I took a day off in Glendive! It's a good thing I didn't add it up until writing that sentence, I'm sure it would have depressed me at the time to think I must keep that pace to make it. The 100 plus mile days were difficult. You go a little batty after 85 miles or so, and I had been racking them up sometimes three days consecutively. I was not sure I could keep that up.

From Jude's Jargon:

On to the Land of 10,000 Lakes!

August 2, 2018

Crossed into Minnesota this morning with little fanfare. I was on a bike path, so no big "Welcome to Minnesota" sign to take a photo of, although Ms. Google Maps gave me a hearty "welcome to Minnesota." Right before crossing over I was on Roger Maris Drive, so I'll give a shout-out to all my sadly misguided Yankee fan friends on the eve of a big weekend series. Today's ride from Fargo to Fergus Falls, MN was good, 60 miles. I did have to dance with Mr. Headwind most of the way, but otherwise, it was pleasant, flat, little to no traffic. I have been tinkering with my routes. I've been using the Adventuring Cycling Route network to guide me home, but yesterday I was playing around with Google Maps and put in Fergus Falls from Fargo. They came up with a route 20 miles shorter than the one I was planning. I tried, and it was great - good roads and conditions. It was especially helpful today as I had 20 miles into a headwind limiting me to 11-12 mph. Probably saved me close to 2 hours in the saddle! I'll continue to make the comparisons because miles saved is a good thing!

Spent the day in Fargo, actually West Fargo, yesterday on a day off. It was pure happenstance, but it turned out to be the perfect day to take off. It was overcast and never got out of the low 60's, plus the wind was howling. It would not have been a pleasant day on the bike. My off days are nice as they give me a chance to recharge and do a few things, namely laundry. They're a good mental break much like leaving work on a Friday knowing you have nothing to get up for on Saturday

161

morning. By the afternoon I usually get a little antsy as I am ready to get going again.

Yesterday after lounging around and waiting for the wash to be done I walked over to Scheels, a sporting goods store near the hotel. This is not just any sporting goods store, it's huge. So big they have a Ferris wheel in the middle which you can ride. Each department devoted to a different sport could have been a store unto itself. There was hockey, baseball, football, golf, hunting, camping, footwear, clothing, everything one could imagine though no lacrosse I could find. They had more guns than I think I've seen in one place, everything from handguns to rifles with some collector's items, such as WWII era Nazi guns, etc. There was also a tremendous number of mounted game trophies. Had I known better I would have studied taxidermy!

Last night for dinner I just went over to the place next to the hotel, Wild Bill's (I went into downtown Fargo the night before). It was an odd combination of sports bar/family restaurant/senior center and casino. They had everything, a blackjack table, numerous TV's all tuned to sports, and there was bingo from 7-9 - seriously - bingo! I sat at the bar as usual. Eventually, two bikers (motorcyclists) came in and sat next to me. They were from Saskatchewan and were members of the Fraternal

162

Order of Eagles out on a little summer excursion. Interesting guys, Randy and Meus (pronounced ME-US), and no, I have no idea what that name is all about! They were both retired, Randy had owned a small trucking company which he sold, and Meus was an electrician. We chatted about various things, and they asked if my ride was for charity. I explained and Randy just handed me twenty bucks and said he didn't need a receipt! Their club is also very charitable, their cause is cystic fibrosis. We talked for a while though we must have appeared an odd group, me with my country club sweatshirt and they with their leather regalia. Meus was particularly decked out with a leather bandanna covering his bald head, the bandanna was embossed with a skull, and he had the proper rings on all fingers and earrings.

It is amazing what people will talk to strangers about. When Meus discovered that I was a lawyer he started in on his lawsuit for medical malpractice. He had had three back surgeries and colorectal cancer. Let's just say he was very descriptive of his issues! He's not the only one who has shared some personal stuff. I ate at a local place the night I stayed in Enderlin. It was Monday so quiet. The few post-work patrons headed out shortly after I arrived. The bartender, who I later discovered was the owner, struck up a conversation. We talked about

163

Enderlin and what people did there. She was from the area but was former military and lived in Bismarck for many years. She and her husband moved to Enderlin and bought the place 3 years earlier and were trying to make a go of it. We discussed the business, their competition, and what she's done for work before. Eventually, she told me that only six months after buying the place her husband had succumbed to PTSD and committed suicide. He had been deployed three times to Kosovo, Iraq, and Afghanistan. It was just so sad. However, she was still plugging away and working hard. I guess it doesn't matter where you are everyone has hurdles to overcome. Deep down, as divided as the country seems, I think we're all just trying to move forward with life and deal with what comes at us every day.

That's about it for me today. Time to find some food. I'm kind of hoping not to run into any interesting people tonight. I'm tired and have a big day tomorrow, plus I want to get back to the room and watch the Sox beat up on the Yanks!

From Jude's Jargon:

Teammates Forever

164

August 5, 2018

It's been a cool few days. I've ridden over 2,100 miles, so over the halfway mark. I estimate I have about 1,600 left, though don't hold me to that, remember words, people words! Have to say so far Minnesota is the most bike friendly state yet. Friday, I rode 83 miles from Fergus Falls to Melrose, seventy-five on bike paths! Then yesterday Melrose to St. Paul 115 miles, first twenty-seven on the path then when I got into Minneapolis it was all paths. By far the easiest city to navigate on a bike so far! Overdid it yesterday, but with good reason. The first four hours of the day I rode in the pouring rain, soaked to the bone. My philosophy - once you're wet it doesn't matter. Not fun, the first real weather I've run into. Back to normal climate - humidity! I needed to get to St. Paul as I was meeting up with a college soccer teammate I haven't seen in over 30 years. The rain stopped, and I still had 70 miles to go, ugh. I kept pushing on, thankfully it was flat. I didn't stop for a proper lunch, survived the day on Coke and Chocolate Chip Cliff bars. My teammate, Beth Lilly, called when I was about 25 miles outside of St. Paul. "Where are you?" "I have no idea," that was our first conversation in 30 years! I explained I was racing my phone battery. I was using Google Maps so needed the phone alive through St. Paul to get me to the hotel. I had stopped earlier at a convenience store to charge it, but my phone wouldn't hold the charge - it had gotten wet during the rain. I stopped earlier and bought sandwich bags to cover it and secured it to the bike with athletic tape - hey, whatever it takes!

I made it to the hotel with 5% battery life to spare! Coming into the Twin Cities was fun, crossed the Mississippi four times. Beth booked me a room at the Intercontinental in St. Paul. That was awesome, the place I stayed at the night before was a total flea bag! They most likely thought I was a vagrant when I got to the Intercontinental. I walked my muddy bike and self into the lobby to check in! Fortunately, I clean up well! Met Beth and her family for dinner and had a blast.

That leads to the deep thought of the day, teammates. I had not seen Beth in over 30 years yet when we saw each other it was as if we never missed a beat. Back in school, she was a senior and captain of the William Smith soccer team, and I was a freshman. We had a great year and spent much time together, playing soccer, studying, etc. The year ended, and she went on to Wall St. while I finished my studies over the next few years. As I planned my trip, I would think about who I knew in various places. I remembered Beth was from St.

Paul. I located her and discovered she was back in Minnesota. When I reached out, she said, "of course, let me know when you're in town."

These are the relationships born on playing fields, or in the production of the school play, or the school band. When you've competed for something day in, and day out with a team you form bonds that remain for life, a common goal, a common existence. You know those friends can be counted on no matter what. Haven't seen or heard from you in 30 years - no worries, whatever you need. It's a very special thing. I've made new friends on this journey and found at least one long ago buddy - hope there will be a few more along the way!

After a great, relaxing night it was time to move on today. I headed to Red Wing, MN about 55 miles from St. Paul. I was feeling yesterday, and even though it wasn't a long ride, it wasn't great. My legs were fried. Got into town around 3:00 and had some time to kick around. Staying in a great, old historic hotel, the St. James. Two nights in a row! I'm spoiled! Found a pub in town and inhaled a pizza. I am finding it hard to eat enough! Certain I will wake up hungry tomorrow. Headed back to the hotel and grabbed a drink at the bar. The woman sitting next to me had worked at the hotel for 48 years - she retired 2 years ago. So interesting to talk to her. She had been there pre and post renovation and worked with one of the original owners. The place was refurbished in the late '70s, beautiful.

168

Being on the Mississippi it wouldn't be right not to have steamboats! Also, Red Wing is home to Red Wing Shoes! Heading further down the river tomorrow toward Iowa where I will cross over and head east across Illinois!

From Jude's Jargon:

On Wisconsin!

August 7, 2018

Leaving Redwing, MN yesterday I hadn't planned to do too much, would go down the Mississippi to Winona, MN, a little over 60 miles. I got to Winona pretty quick, it was only 1:00 p.m., so I headed down another 30 miles to Lacrosse, Wisconsin. It was a nice ride down route 61, right along the river with rolling hills. What wind there was was at my back, so it felt good to keep going. I went through some lovely small towns that sit right on the river. At one point I saw signs for Pepin Lake. Frankly, it still looked like the river to me. I stopped in Wabasha to get a drink and talked to a man at the service station. He cycled a little himself and had lots of questions. We got to talking about the area, and he told me to keep an eye out for eagles. He said it was funny, photographers would show up with their huge lens's looking for the eagles flying over the lake. Apparently often, unbeknownst to the photographers, the eagles would be flying over their heads behind them. When he mentioned the lake, I said "time out - straighten this out for me. You're saying there's actually a lake within the river??" "Well, it's three miles wide at that point so yes." Who knew that the Mississippi was a multi-tasker!

Last night I stayed in Lacrosse, WI. For dinner, I found a nice place in town, Houghton's - Jackson St. Pub. The owner was behind the bar training a new bartender. I'm easy to pick out as an out-of-towner due to my tan. Trust me I put on sunscreen every morning but 6-8 hours outside every day has left its mark. Anyway, Keith the owner remarked on it, and I explained what I was doing. He has lived in the area for many years though is originally from Iowa. We discussed routes, and he was very helpful, to the point he got out his laptop, and we looked at some route alternatives. Turns out he and his wife bought the restaurant two years ago. It has been there for many years but needed some new blood. It had catered to an older crowd, they wanted to spice things up. There's a dining room and a separate pub which was quite nice. Keith loved owning the place and making it his own. He added the "Jackson St. Pub" to the name so people in town knew there was a change and out-of-towners like me might find it. He proudly declared that they had doubled revenue since taking over. He should work for the Chamber of Commerce; he gave me an overview of what makes Lacrosse hum - big medical and several colleges. The food was great and the conversation even better.

I decided that today would be a shorter ride as I was on my 6th straight day. Over those days I rode through four states, N. Dakota, Minnesota, Wisconsin, and Iowa, covering 470 miles. Time for a rest day tomorrow! Today's ride was beautiful as well, down the east side of the river on Rte. 35 from Lacrosse to Marquette, Iowa. The weather was perfect, overcast and cool, no wind. Again, it was gently rolling hills so not tough. I felt it was my sixth day in a row though. It's like that last run of the day when you're skiing, your legs are tired, and you probably should have quit a little earlier, but you just need to finish. The last 10 miles were trying. The truck traffic was picking up, and that generally stresses me out. The road was fine and had a good shoulder, but you can hear them coming, just not fun when you're tired.

My new assistant navigator, Keith, tells me I will have to deal with some "buttes" as I ride down the river in Iowa. Buttes, merely a quaint name for hills! I don't like hills or buttes either for that matter! So, it's good to have a day off to rest the legs and my butt! I would imagine you are all wondering about the "butt!" It's fine but a lot of days in a row do take a toll!

From Jude's Jargon:

Don't Your Wheels Fall Off When You Ride That Far???

August 10, 2018

It's been an uneventful few days out here. Spent the off day doing some laundry and looking at routes for the upcoming days. I did have a special treat on my day off, I made a video call to the kids at the Providence Boys & Girls Clubs. They were great and had lots of questions.

172

"What do I eat? Where do I stay? are there pools at the hotels? What kind of animals have I seen?" The best by far was from a young boy, "Don't your wheels fall off when you ride that far?" Not sure if he meant that literally or figuratively, certainly my mental wheels have been in danger of coming off on some trying days! Hopefully, I'll get to chat with them again before I'm done.

Navigator Keith was right about Iowa, I had some buttes to contend with. Them buttes were beauts! I felt like I was back in eastern Oregon for a while there yesterday. They were steep but happily not that long. Yesterday was a tough one, the climbs were tough, and it was low 90's and very humid. I did 60 miles from Marquette to Dubuque; it was a hard sixty. Took me three and a half hours to do 30 miles, contrast that with the other day from Redwing to Lacrosse when I did the first 60 miles in just over four hours. Crazy! I spent that day, and today too, surrounded by corn. It's everywhere! The last 5 miles into Dubuque were on a nice bike path. Usually, bike paths are scenic. We're especially spoiled in RI with the East Bay path that runs along Narragansett Bay. I had to laugh yesterday as I rode by a clearing and looked over to see, what else, more corn! I swear every available spit of land has corn on it. Whatever they use

173

for fertilizer is not so pleasant, it's putrid. Between the hills, the heat, the humidity and the smell I was nauseous.

Checked out Dubuque, nice little city. Dropped Crazy Horse off at a shop for a little TLC. She was fine, just wanted to make sure everything was looking good for the push home. The bike shop owner was yet another great person. I dropped the bike off at 3:00 p.m. he said he'd try to get to it before he closed at 6:00. He called just before 6:00 and said it was ready, but he was leaving in about 10 minutes. However, he said he would be in early today, so I could get going. He texted at 8:00 a.m. and said he was at the shop even though they don't open til 10:00. He didn't want to delay my day!

Today was better as the humidity and temps were down some and the climbs not as tough. Though I did get treated to a hot flash during a climb with the sun beating down on me! Ain't life grand? The shop owner had helped with my route too. I had planned to go down the east side of the river through Galena, Ill. Having just finished Ron Chernow's new biography of Ulysses Grant I wanted to see the town he called home. I was dissuaded when I heard that to get to Galena the climbs would be like yesterday. He didn't have to tell me twice!

As I said uneventful. Got to take more bike trails today. I was literally riding through farmland with nothing around but the occasional farmhouse, just me and the corn. Suddenly the Google Maps app said turn right, so I did. There was a bike path, appearing out of nowhere. I guess if you build it in Iowa, they will come!

A few general musings. North Dakota and Minnesota get the Broadway thing - just Broadway, not St. or Ave. Unfortunately, Iowa does not. I passed a Broadway St. yesterday. I had such high hopes for Iowa! I mean really, weren't those standardized tests we took in grade school called the "Iowa tests"??? Both ND and MN have Heineken though I have found none in Iowa yet! Iowa is a Pepsi state; Coke's are few and far between. Do you think they had a statewide referendum?? I think it's still "pop" here, but my spirits were lifted when I saw a sign for "soda" in a store window.

That's all for now. Heading out of Iowa into Illinois in the morning. I have estimated that I should be home 3 weeks from today - I can't believe the end is in sight!

From Jude's Jargon:

Why Did They Put That Sign There?? OOOh, That's Why!

August 12, 2018

It's been a long couple of days, I'd have to put yesterday in top five of bad days on the trip. I knew it would be a long one, 103 miles from Clinton, Iowa to Oglesby, Illinois. I didn't expect it to be as trying as it was. The first 45 miles were nice. Crossed the Mississippi for the last time and rode into Illinois. It was farmland and some gently rolling hills. There was no one on the road, it was peaceful. Apparently, they don't use the same fertilizer as they do in Iowa, it smelled just fine! My route took me onto the Hennepin Canal Trail. I was on it for 35-40 miles, it was bad. In parts it was paved but lots of gravel on the pavement, then it would narrow into a dirt path with long grass which got pushed aside by my panniers, then it would revert to a gravel path. It went on and on and on, a struggle. There were several tunnels which took you under roads. I got to the first which was short, maybe 15 yards. There was a sign reading "walk bikes through tunnel." Hmm, couldn't figure out why so I rode right through no problem. I got to the second one same thing, again rode right through. I got to the third, same sign. I started in, but this one was longer. 40 yards or so. It got dark really fast even though I could see the light at the end. There were also some nasty ruts which I couldn't see. About half way through I figured out why the sign was there as I was getting tossed around in the dark. Couldn't get out of my pedals quick enough so crash! So that's why they want you to walk your bike! Got a few scrapes but fine, though it didn't help my attitude about the path much! And I did walk through the next one!

The day got no better. I finally got off the path, bruised, battered and dusty, I stopped to get a snack and a drink. It was hot 90-92, so I had been drinking a lot all day. I only had 20 miles to go it couldn't be that bad right?? Well, Illinois doesn't seem to believe in shoulders for their roads so any time I was near a town or city, I felt exposed. I continued, being directed by Google Maps. It took me off the main road which could have been good but turned bad quickly when it became a rugged, gravelly, dirt road. You must be kidding me!!! That was the last thing I needed right then! Perhaps my wheels would fall off. It lasted about 4 miles but took a toll on me. Those roads are hard on your upper body as you're stressed trying to make sure your back wheel doesn't skid out behind you. Finally pulled into the hotel, 9.5 hours after I began. I had a pizza delivered and went to sleep!

This morning I vowed not to go on a "trail" today. I selected the Google route which would avoid them. Being the idiot I am, I misread the directions out of the hotel and 3 miles later ended up at the trail head for the Illinois - Michigan Canal Trail (the I&M). Aaarrgh! The alternative was to retrace my route and get back on the other route - we know there's no going back so I guess the I&M would happen. Thankfully, it was much better than the Hennepin. Most of it was hard pack dirt with no gravel so an easier ride. It did get narrow for a time, and I had to get over a few fallen trees. It was flat and shaded, a plus since it was another hot one. I was on the trail for about 40 miles. Poor Crazy Horse is quite dusty too! Ten of my last 15 miles were on the Kanakee River Trail, the best one yet, shady and well paved! I got into tonight's destination, after 85 hot miles, at about 4:00 p.m. Staying in Bourbonnais, Ill., summer home of Da Bears! I know I must be getting close to home. There's a Dunkin Donuts here! On to Indiana tomorrow!

The day I fell in the tunnel was just awful. Looking back on it I would rank in the top three of bad days. It was super-hot, and the fall didn't help matters much. You know it can't be good when the first thought while lying on your side in a dark tunnel in the middle of "somewhere" Illinois is "I wonder if its broken?" meaning the arm I had just landed on. I didn't share that on the blog at the time because I didn't want people to worry. There was a deep scratch on my forearm, and it was bruised. I still have a scar four months later. I hope it doesn't go away, it's a good reminder.

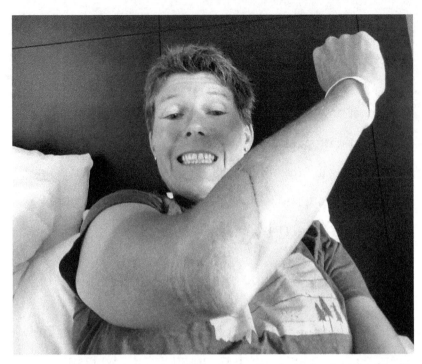

After getting out of the tunnel, I brushed myself off and stopped for a few minutes. I was a little light headed and don't think I'd eaten enough, so I had a cliff bar and some water in the shade. There were still 50 miles to go, and I honestly don't know how I got through it. After dealing with the unforeseen dirt road, which just downright sucked, I was only about 20 miles from my destination. I stopped at a traffic light in a small town and a convertible TR-6, vintage 1978, pulled up next to me. The top was down, and the woman in the passenger seat asked if I wanted to race. If I hadn't laughed, I would have cried. They were very nice. It was a long light, so we chatted for a few minutes.

I'm sure Illinois is a lovely state and some good friends hale from there, however, it was not a great experience on a bike. I'm skeptical about how they qualify what a "bike path" is. Rhode Island offers wonderful paths, and I traversed many through Minnesota and New York State which were excellent. I guess that's just part of the adventure!

My evening in Bourbonnais, Ill. was great though. The restaurant next to the hotel was Italian, Tucci's. Being from the Providence area I am spoiled when it comes to Italian food, we have some of the best in the United States.

I had been reticent to try Italian thus far, though I hadn't had many opportunities. Tucci's was different, I could tell when I walked in the door. It had that bustle and hum of activity that most good restaurants do. I became convinced it would be good when I opened the menu and there was a reference to "gravy" rather than sauce. For the uninitiated, Italians, at least those in RI, refer to their red sauce as gravy. I didn't want you to think they were putting turkey gravy over pasta!

I sat at the bar as always and inhaled some delicious chicken parmesan. It was a Sunday night so quiet. An older gentleman sat down near me at the bar. He had just finished dinner with several of his adult children and was treating himself to an after-dinner drink. He ordered a black coffee with sambuca on the side. This caught my attention, that's what my Dad would drink after dinner every night. We struck up a nice conversation. He lost his first wife and remarried a few years ago. Between them, they had a boatload of kids and grandkids. The bartender joined in on the conversation after a bit, and we learned he was studying to be a nurse. He was an ambitious young man and very amiable, I'm sure he will make a great nurse.

After a nice evening fortified with good food and conversation, I ready to take on Indiana the next day. The states were coming quickly now. It had only taken me two days to get through Illinois. I had a short day the next day to get to Rennselaer, IN so I could do laundry and rest up.

Nicole and Mary Anne for the Boys & Girls Clubs of Providence were coming out for the day on Tuesday. I think they wanted to make sure my psychological wheels hadn't fallen off! Nicole had the canny ability to text me at the worst possible moments. The day I was heading into St. Paul in the pouring rain. "How are you doing?" popped up on my phone. "Besides getting poured on fine."

"I love St. Paul" she replied.

I was not in a mood to love anything just then. Or the day I was fighting a strong headwind into Custer, Montana.

"Hey, do you want to coach the swim team at the club this fall?"

"Now would not be a good time to ask me to do anything!" She meant well, but her timing sucked.

From Jude's Jargon:

Closer to Home

August 16, 2018

It's been quite an eventful few days since I last checked in with all of you! Got a little distracted and out of sync with my usual routine. Back on track today so let me fill you in. I left off in Bourbonnais, Illinois and had yet another indication I was closer to home. I walked over to

183

the Italian restaurant next to the hotel. I knew right away it would be good - menu referred to gravy rather than sauce! Yes!! I had images of Federal Hill rolling through my brain!

The next day, Monday, I had a short hop into Rennselaer, Indiana, 50 miles. It was uneventful, just more flat farmland. I turned onto a new road, and Google welcomed me to Indiana. At least someone is celebrating with me! Riding through rural Indiana is like riding on a chess board. Go straight for five miles, turn left and continue for two miles, turn right go another five miles, and so on and so on. The roads are all dead straight, so all your turns are 90 degrees. The scenery is the same, corn, corn and more corn. The roads are good except when they inexplicably go from paved to dirt then back again. It would be nice to know who makes those decisions - let's pave these 10 miles then we'll skip a mile and a half then pave again.

Got to the hotel early and wanted to get some lunch. It was surrounded by fast food, Arby's, KFC, etc. which didn't interest me. I asked the clerk at the hotel if there was anywhere else around to eat. She said "not really, it would be another 5 miles to ride into Rennselaer" which didn't appeal to me either. "Uber?" She laughed "definitely not." I headed to Arby's and then

184

went over to the gas station to get some laundry detergent and beer - figured it would be a pizza in the room night. I discovered that Indiana has an interesting law on beer sales. I went over to the cooler and saw wine but no beer. Asked the clerk if they had cold beer. Nope, they're not allowed to sell cold beer. Hence, they had only warm twelve packs. Good thing my room had a fridge! I have probably made the housekeeping staff at several places happy when they discovered what was left in my fridge!

Tuesday was a day off and Nicole and Mary Anne, the CEO and Development Director at the Boys & Girls Clubs of Prov., flew in to spend the day. I think they wanted to make sure my wheels were still secure! We had a nice afternoon and evening checking out

185

Rennselaer and the surrounding area. It was nice to get chauffeured around for a change and not have to walk or pedal to dinner! The next day they gave me a boost and drove me part way along my route on their way to the airport, so I didn't have a full 90-mile day. My legs were thankful!

Last night I met up with another long-lost friend, Mike Auger and his wife Cathi, in Warsaw, IN. They drove down from their home in Elkhart about a half hour away. We determined we probably hadn't seen each other since his sister's wedding almost 30 years ago! Cathi was a rock star to put up with our Rumford reminiscing! It was a nice respite and great to see a familiar face along the way!

I headed out this morning for Defiance, Ohio, check the box on another state! Google and I celebrated alone again when I crossed the border - no one even put up a sign to welcome me and Crazy Horse! It was a perfect day for a ride, overcast, maybe 80 degrees, no wind and not a "bike path" in sight! I did the 85 miles in about 6.5 hours. I did get rained on for the last hour, but it was light. The clerks at the Holiday Inn had a good chuckle when I walked in soaking wet!

I'm feeling closer to home, into the Eastern Time Zone yesterday! By my calculations I have less than 900 miles to go - though remember - I do words! I'm still on track to be home the week of the 27th - not sure what day yet!

In Rensselaer, I figured I was only about two weeks from home. I could not believe I'd been on the road for six weeks. It felt like I'd come a long way and indeed I had, 2,800 miles, only about 1,000 more. Seemed like nothing right?? My mind set was changing. I think it was because I was getting into the east. Once I crossed into Ohio, I would be on familiar ground, especially when I got into New York, having driven back and forth to Hobart & William Smith Colleges from RI for years as a student and an alum.

I was also ready to be home. The daily routine of hotel breakfast, consisting of bowls of Raisin Bran and bagels, riding 80-100 miles to the next hotel, finding dinner, sleeping and getting up to do it again the next day was getting old! Plus, I missed my dog terribly!

Since I had only two weeks to go, I figured I might as well lighten the load. I packed up my two front panniers to send home with Nicole and Mary Anne. I was in more densely populated areas with no threat of getting stranded in the high desert with not a soul around for many miles. If I needed anything, I could buy it.

Do I Really Want To Come Back To This?

August 17, 2018

I suppose it was bound to happen, back to reality. I was having such a nice morning. My ride was going well, 70 miles from Defiance to Fremont, Ohio. It was flat with no wind, even the first 45 minutes of light rain weren't bothering me. I was 45-50 miles in coming through Bowling Green, a pleasant town. Up ahead of me was a four-way stop sign, it was flat, and there was little traffic so I could see what was going on. I slowed as I approached, the only other car was approaching from the left. I arrived at the intersection about a second before the car. I slowed to an almost complete stop, basically as slow as I could go without falling over as my feet were clipped in. I checked the intersection as the car to my left came to a stop. I started pedaling through. The guy in the car beeped and heatedly pointed to the stop sign. Seriously Dude???? Okay maybe I didn't obey the exact letter of the law, but I certainly acted within the spirit of it. I didn't brazenly fly through the intersection at 15 mph, my average speed for the day, I slowed to a virtual stop and having the right of way continued.

Frankly, if I stopped, unclipped and then went he would have been held up longer!

I'd gone from relaxed to annoyed in a heartbeat, and it stunk. Yesterday I had Amish ladies waving at me from their buggies, today I was beeped at by an overly righteous jerk. What's been great about this whole trip is the relaxed nature and just general niceness of everyone I've met and seen. Farmers wave at me from their tractors. People engage in conversation outside gas stations; curious to know where I'm going and where I've been. There's no judging, no contempt, no animosity. I'm going back to my theory of a few weeks ago - rural America is more relaxed because people are not on top off each other all the time. Your neighbors don't know your every move, nor do they care. There's space to breath and relax. Not everyone is in a huge rush just to have to stop at the next traffic light.

If this journey has done anything for me, I'm hoping I stay more relaxed. There are more important things to worry about than what everyone else is doing!

Loving Ohio!

August 20, 2018

As I am moving on to Pennsylvania and New York tomorrow, I have to say I thoroughly enjoyed the few days I spent in Ohio. The riding was nice, good roads, flat terrain, and little wind. Although I was riding from 75 to 90 miles a day, it wasn't taxing. Perhaps I'm just in shape now! Over the weekend and today, I spent most of my time riding along Lake Erie. On Saturday I started in Fremont and went up to Huron to get on Rte. 6 and head eastward along the lake shore. It was beautiful with some gorgeous homes along the lake. Cleveland proved easy to navigate on the bike, though being Saturday probably helped. I was excited to get there as a close college friend, Meg McIntosh, was driving up from Columbus to spend Saturday night with me. She's familiar with the city, so I had a tour guide. We had a great evening relaxing and catching up!

Meg had to get going on Sunday morning, but I decided to take the day off, hang around town and catch an Indians game. It may be the only game I get to this summer, so I splurged and got a great seat about four rows behind the first base dugout.

I love baseball especially going to the games. No matter what stadium you're in the vibe is the same. You get onto the concourse and fans are flowing in both directions. You smell the sausage and onions cooking, the popcorn and beer. There's pregame electricity as the fans find their seats. How will the boys do today? There are hopes for a win. Going from under the stadium out to the stands is always such a wonderful experience. You emerge from a sea of people surrounded by concrete into the sunlit stadium with its pristine infield and grass. The pace of the game has a life of its own with no clocks or whistles to worry about. The hum of the crowd is constant, ebbing and flowing with the play on the field.

My love of the game comes from my parents, they were both huge fans. My mother turned 13 in 1939 the year Ted Williams joined the Red Sox. She thought he was the most handsome thing. Her brother would listen to the games on the radio every afternoon, and sometimes her father would take them up to Boston on the train from Providence to catch a game. All her life she could rattle off those 30's and 40's lineups, Williams, Pesky, Doerr, DiMaggio - Dom, not that other one who played for the Yankees. She lamented later in life that it was frustrating to keep up with the team as the lineups changed so much from season to season.

My Dad was a player and a fan. I'll never forget the time right before my high school graduation when he relayed this experience. We are standing on the steps of the library at Vermont Academy and he harkened back to a day in June exactly 40 years prior. He had stood on those same steps with two letters in his hand. One was from the Boston Braves asking him to come to Braves field for a tryout, the second was also a draft notice. Seeing it was June 1944 you might imagine what the second notice was. The Braves would have to take a backseat to the war.

Yesterday was perfect for baseball in Cleveland, sunny, low 80's. I gathered up my hot dog and beer and found my way to my seat. I sat next to Al, a truck driver from Huron, who had also purchased a single ticket. We had a lovely time chatting. He was a follower of the Indians, but Ohio State football is his real love. He explained his sister had had Indians season tickets for years, but sadly she had just died of pancreatic cancer. Damned disease - I hate it! He's driven all over the country for work and had been to Fenway a few times. He added that he wouldn't be going through RI anytime soon as he had heard about the new truck tolls. "You have a minor league team too, right?" he asked.

"Well, we used to..." I'm so sad about that, but it's a story for another day. He had visions of his own journey which he relayed after learning what I was doing. He wants to take his boat through the lakes on down the Erie Canal to the Hudson then down the Intracoastal to Florida. Told him it sounded great and to do it sooner than later!

The Indians won; I was happy for them. I was their fan for a day. Tonight, they're in Boston, so I'll have to root against them, oh well.

It's on to NY State tomorrow, and it's almost a little bittersweet. I'll be in familiar territory and will lose some of the sense of adventure I've had until now, but it also means I'm inching ever closer to home! I have about 650 miles left which seem like nothing at this point! I've already traveled some 3,100! Planning to be back a week from Wednesday barring any unforeseen happenings!

THE FINAL STRETCH

As I left Ohio and passed through Erie, Pa. along Lake Erie and on into New York State, I sensed things accelerating. I would be home in a week. Something which not many days before had been hard to comprehend. Now the mission was to keep plugging away. It was easy to think I was close to home, but I still had over 600 miles to pedal. The best part of this stretch would be staying with familiar faces, I would only be in hotels a few nights across NY State.

I reflected on the things I'd seen. People often asked along the route what my favorite place or experience was. Until this point, I hadn't thought about it. Every day when I finished my thoughts were on the next day. What my route would be? Where would I stay? What was the weather forecast? I believe it was this constant push forward, and homeward that kept me going. As I write this, months later, I'm in awe of the distances I rode, day after day. A hundred miles one day, ninety-eight the next then another ninety-five the day after that, it just didn't stop. Perhaps, had I thought much about it at the time I would have realized how crazy it was and it wouldn't have been so easy to get up and keep going the next day.

It was riding along Lake Erie then Lake Ontario and the Niagara River that started me thinking about what I'd seen in just two short months. I'd begun on the sands of the Pacific coast, climbed the Cascades following the Lewis & Clark Trail through the Rocky Mountains and across the Continental Divide. I'd ridden for miles along the Yellowstone River then across the Missouri River into the Land of 10,000 Lakes before hitting the head of the Mississippi and riding alongside it for days through Minnesota, Wisconsin, and Iowa. Once I left the Mississippi behind it was onto the cornfields of the mid-west and the Great Lakes. Heading east from Buffalo and Lake Ontario I traveled along one of America's first man-made wonders, the Erie Canal. Following it for hundreds of miles, then across the Hudson River and into the Berkshires of Western Massachusetts. Finally, I would get to my little home state of Rhode Island, traveling from the slightly rolling terrain in the western part of the state into downtown Providence and the head of Narragansett Bay leading out to the Atlantic.

It is overwhelming to think about all those sights and places and imagine what I had achieved. Many Americans may only see one or two of these wonders in their lifetime, or perhaps none. I recalled the young boy at the Oregon Hotel in Mitchell, OR set to graduate high school the next year. He was planning to stay in Mitchell, population 130, and work for his family. I wanted to shake him by the shoulders and tell him to go see the world. You can always go back! It blows my mind to think I'd seen and experienced all these things in just two months and from the seat of a bicycle!

Though these reflections entered my thoughts, I still had a week to go. It was a week of ups and downs to be sure. My first night in western NY was in Dunkirk, right on Lake Ontario. I spent the day getting there from Conneaut, Ohio, mainly dodging weather systems. I got lucky and had to endure only a few light showers, though it was hot. Once I got into Dunkirk, the weather came through. There was even a tornado warning for the next county over. I was glad to finish and watch the storm roll off the lake from the hotel.

The next day I was on to Grand Island, just north of Buffalo across the Niagara River. I was excited as I only had about 57 miles to get there and would be staying with great friends, Karen and Barry Smith. Karen's brother Pete is a close friend in RI I had visited the Smith's several times before. I must have been distracted because I rode the first 8 miles that day without my helmet. I reached up and unthinkingly ran my fingers through my hair. "Hmm," I thought, "that feels weird." It took a second for it to dawn on me I didn't have my helmet on! Thankfully it was right there atop my rear panniers where I always put it when I'm off the bike. The rest of the ride was mundane. The only annoyance was that my cell phone kept restarting when I got into Buffalo. This was a problem because I was using Google Maps to get me to the Smith's house so every time it restarted I had to stop and reset it. I didn't realize how alarmed Karen was at the same time. I had linked her on Glimpse in the morning so she could follow my progress to their house. Once the phone reset it kicked her off the app. I didn't think about it at the time, but she was worried that something had happened! Oops. We concluded the phone was alternately pinging off towers in the U.S. and Canada making the software shut down.

I got to the house and she and Scotch, their golden retriever, were there to greet me. It was so nice to relax in a real home. After showering, I did laundry and caught up with Karen. They had planned a friendly little gathering for that evening. Barry had made his famous meatballs, and

Pete and Karen's mother, sister, and a few friends were coming over. It was great hanging out and catching up with everyone. The meatballs were great though my stomach hadn't felt right all day. I didn't think much of it; however, that would change from 2:00 a.m. on! I was up about every hour. Not a great night's sleep. Karen made me some excellent French toast for breakfast. It tasted great, so I figured last night was behind me, and all would be fine.

From Jude's Jargon:

Gorgeous Day on the Erie Canal

August 23, 2018

After spending the last few days dodging weather systems today was spectacular for a ride along the Erie Canal, bright sun, temps in the 70's, flat with a tailwind. Add that seventy of my 88 miles were along the Erie Canal Trailway and it's a perfect day! It's been a good week. Headed out of Conneaut, Ohio on Tuesday and rode through Erie, Pa and into New York, wrapping up the day in Dunkirk. Three states in one day - I must be in the northeast! Took route 5 right along Lake Erie so had more great scenery. I was greeted by 8 miles of "grooved pavement" in NY. My teeth are getting looser by the day - poor Crazy Horse, she's putting up with some tough terrain! Got into Dunkirk ahead of the weather. We had a storm blow through around 5, there were tornado warnings to the southeast - yikes! The wind had been howling from the south, a good 20-25 mph all day. Luckily that direction didn't hurt me as I was heading northeast.

Yesterday I hopped to Grand Island, NY, just across the Niagara River from Buffalo to spend the evening with the Hayes/Smith clan. It was great - my first home cooked meal in a long time! Barry's famous meatballs and pasta! After a great evening of food and conversation and a good night's sleep, I was off to Rochester this morning. As I mentioned the other day I'm heading into familiar territory, western and central New York having gone to school in Geneva, NY, Hobart and William Smith Colleges. Over the last 35 years, I've spent a lot of time traversing the area from campus to home and many bus rides throughout the state to soccer and lacrosse games. The names are so familiar, Lockport, Brockport, Rochester, Syracuse, Oneonta, Hamilton, but I'm seeing them in a whole new light. A gentleman in Montana suggested that "When you travel by car, you see what man made. When you travel by horse, you see what God made."

I will include Crazy Horse in the horse category. Not sure who created what but seeing the country through this perspective is entirely different than traveling by car. You get to see stuff because you're not traveling at 80 miles an hour enclosed in metal and glass. You feel and experience your surroundings, it's nice. You stop in places you wouldn't be likely to in a car, and you interact with many more people.

People often ask me if I listen to anything while I ride. When I ride at home I often listen to podcasts so I can hear the traffic noise too. I thought about it before embarking on the journey but decided against it for several reasons. When I started out west the roads were narrow and shoulders slim, so I had to be cognizant of traffic. I could not afford to get distracted when eighteen-wheel logging trucks were blowing by me at 60-70 mph. Then I discovered that I just enjoyed the quiet and taking in the scenery. It was just so cool to be going through the route Lewis and Clark took to the coast. It was fun to imagine them seeing it for the first time just as I was. It was the same today on the canal. It was so calm and pristine. I just wanted to imagine the barges going up and down being dragged along by horses on the "towpath" now a bike path. The scenery was great, great blue herons taking off from the reeds as I approached, loons popping their heads up here and there. I just didn't want to spoil it by distracting myself with music or a podcast.

That's about it for today. I'm in Rochester and the signs of my approach to home become more abundant - today I passed by a Friendly's Ice Cream Shop and a Dunkin Donuts!! See you all next week!

Once I settled into my room in Rochester, I headed out to get dinner. Thankfully there was a brick oven pizza place next door to the hotel. I walked over and sat at the bar as usual. My stomach was fine all day, though I had eaten little. I know, I know, probably foolish to ride almost 90 miles without eating more than a cliff bar and a couple of Cokes, but I did it so can't take it back. I got a small pizza figuring the cheese and dough would be helpful. It tasted great, so I downed the whole thing.

After dinner, I headed back to the room to catch the Red Sox game and some sleep. Everything was great until I woke up about an hour after turning in, uh oh! Yup, I was up again all night. A horrible experience. I probably should have taken the next day off, but I was on a mission to get to Syracuse where I would stay with my close friends and college buddies, Adair and Patrick Milmoe. I was not to be deterred. Besides, it was Friday, and I was planning to take the next day off to spend with them.

I got up and had breakfast which tasted good, so I set off on my 88-mile trek. I got back on the Canal Trail and followed it toward Syracuse. Adair was meeting me at the Erie Canal Museum later that afternoon. She would drive me south to their home in Cazenovia. It was a good day for a ride with temps in the low 80's. I would be on and off canal path all day. It was fun once I got to the area around Geneva, going through all the towns which had once only been names on interstate signs. I would have liked to stop in Geneva and catch up with some friends at the Colleges, however, it would have taken me 30 miles off route. I decided against it.

After getting off the Canal Trail in Clyde I found myself on some beautiful country roads, going through farmland and rolling hills. For those of you who think of New York as a city, you should get out and explore the rest of it. It's spectacularly beautiful. I came upon another cyclist by the side of the road. He was also touring so I stopped to chat. Turns out he'd just changed a flat and was getting ready to head out again. He was recently retired and getting into bicycle touring. He was out for the weekend and didn't live far from where we were. He asked lots of questions about touring and was surprised when I told him it was my first trip. It is a little weird that I had never even done an overnight before setting out on a 4,000-mile journey, but hey how hard is it to just ride a bike?? I suppose by the time I ran into him I was experienced having ridden just shy of 3,500 miles.

We said our goodbyes and I continued on, winding my way through the countryside. It was hot, and I was feeling the poor quality of the last two night's sleep and the dearth of food. I had another seven or eight miles to go to get to the museum, and my body was screaming at me. My "just keep going" mantra was wearing a little thin. I came around a bend in the road and confronted a hill. It wasn't a huge hill, but it was enough to purely deflate me. Fortunately, there was a fork in the road, and the right turn led downhill to a commercial area. I stopped for a few seconds to decide which way to go. The downhill won, and I cruised down to a Costco parking lot to call Adair.

Whadda Ya Got In Here? A Dead Body???

August 26, 2018

Limped into Syracuse Friday afternoon after two 85-mile plus days from Grand Island. Some intestinal issues causing two nights of poor sleep and a little dehydration didn't help matters. Fortunately, I was taking a much-needed day off Saturday and staying with old, dear college friends Adair and Patrick Milmoe in Cazenovia. Got to a Costco outside of Syracuse and waited for Adair to pick me up for the ride to Cazenovia, about 30 minutes south of the city. I have to say people watching outside Costco on a Friday afternoon rivals a good day at the airport!

Adair pulled up and helped me get my stuff into the SUV. She picked up one of my panniers and exclaimed, "Whadda ya got in there? A dead body???" There's my Long Island girl!! Too funny, but seriously the only easy time dealing with my gear is when I'm riding. Maneuvering the bike with panniers through hotels and elevators isn't an easy thing to do. My legs are always sporting scratches and bruises from banging into the bike, or maybe the bike banging into me!

We pulled into the driveway of their 19th-century farmhouse and were greeted by Charlotte, the St. Bernard, and George, the Cocker Spaniel, an unlikely duo but the best of buddies. I could instantly feel myself relax; this was just what I needed. I'd known these two since we were freshmen in college, and I'd spent many evenings with them in Cazenovia. It was the next best thing to home. These are friends that no matter how long it's been since you've seen one another you just pick right up as if it was yesterday. They'd just become empty nesters as their youngest went off to college a few days ago, so we had the place to ourselves. We hung out, relaxed and laughed for two days.

After two good night's sleep, my stomach was back to normal. It was time to shove off this morning. The final push is on! Four more riding days and I'm home! Patrick had to run into his office this morning in Canastota, so he dropped me at the Erie Canalway Trail which runs right through town. Crazy Horse was raring to go! She got a new front shoe yesterday and was feeling good. I probably could have made it home with the old tire, but it gave me peace of mind to change it. The last thing I need is to spend the next four days worrying about it. I'd changed her chain last week, so she's running perfectly right now!

Had an uneventful ride up to Herkimer, 52 miles, much of it on the canal bikeway. It took me over a working lock, cool. The other thing that's been nice following this trail is going through towns and cities previously only words on a Thruway sign. Herkimer, Utica, Rome, Port Byron, Clyde became real. Home is becoming more than just a word for me too. I can't believe as I write this, I will have only three more rides to get into Providence! It's on to Albany tomorrow, then Springfield and finally Providence Wednesday, unbelievable. I've ridden over 3,500 miles!

I learned that Senator John McCain died yesterday. Many people tell me they are awed by my determination and perseverance in doing this ride. However, I can't hold a candle to the late Senator, a true American hero. It's hard to imagine spending five years in a North Vietnamese prison camp being repeatedly tortured. Makes my journey seem like a day in the park.

He was a man of integrity and honor, a patriot and a hero. Rest in peace Senator, rest in peace.

HOMEWARD BOUND

I left Herkimer the morning of the 27th excited because I had only three more days to ride. It was unbelievable I was almost done; however, my mind was not relaxed as there was still riding to do!

I spent that evening in Clifton Park, NY with my cousin Phil and his wife, Brigette. Once again it was great to be in a relaxed place and not worry about finding a hotel or deciding where to eat. Phil asked if I had any special dinner requests. After thinking about it, I asked for a simple steak and corn on the cob. I hadn't had a good steak during the whole trip, though it wasn't as if I was going to high-end restaurants. I'd also spent the last half of the trip riding

208

through endless cornfields and passing numerous roadside stands. It was like floating in the ocean surrounded by water and not being able to drink a drop of it! Besides there's nothing like native, steamed corn on the cob, smothered in butter with a bit of salt. My mouth waters as I write this.

It was a low-key evening we sat around the dinner table catching up. Brigette told the story of her own extraordinary journey climbing Mt. Kilimanjaro. I never knew she did that, though I wasn't surprised, she's a great athlete and a great skier. Phil asked if I wanted to stick around and take a day off to play golf. I begged off as I was too close to home to think about stopping now.

The next day Phil dropped me back on the route around 8:00 a.m. It was already warm and promised to be one of the hottest days of the summer, mid-90's for sure., Knowing it would be hot and long and hilly, I was cautious about the day. I planned on 90 miles through the Berkshires, ouch! I had seen little in the way of hills since eastern Iowa, and that was eons ago. The Berkshires are nothing like the Cascades or the Rockies, but they are mountains!

I rode south along the Hudson for a while on Rte. 9J. It was nice and flat until I turned east and headed out of the river valley, facing a steep climb. It would be the first of several sessions pushing Crazy Horse uphill that day. I thought the Berkshires would be a piece of cake, after all, I was in cycling shape. I had also ditched my front panniers and lost about 15-20 lbs. All of which should have made it easier. But it didn't. My legs were just plain fried from riding over 3,600 miles to date. The heat wasn't helping much either.

At the top of that climb I stopped at a gas station to get some Gatorade, I'd ridden only 8 miles over 44 minutes. Soaked with sweat, I was already gassed. This would be a long day. My challenge was hydration as the liquid was coming out of me as fast as it was going in. I drank at least a quart of Gatorade at every stop that day and water while I was riding. Not sure how much I drank, but I should have bought Gatorade stock before leaving on the trip!

A little after noon I crossed into Massachusetts which gave me a much-needed mental boost as temps were in the mid-90's with high humidity. This was nothing like riding through the dry heat of the west, it was more like slicing your way through a wet mass of air. I reached a

Subway restaurant and wolfed down a footlong steak and cheese with some chips, coke and more Gatorade. My clothes were so soaked I could have wrung them out. I had to wipe down the puddle I left on my seat in the restaurant! The disheartening thing was I had only traveled 35 miles and still had fifty-five to go, and it was already close to 1:00 p.m. This would be a hell of a day.

The food and drink helped with my energy, and my next stint was another 35 miles. It was a hard leg though with hills and traffic on Rte. 20. I was using Google Maps and when possible, it got me off the main road while keeping me in the right direction, avoiding traffic. This could be good and bad. During this stretch I went off Rte. 20, it was great until I was directed onto a dirt road! I was pissed off. I thought my days of dirt had ended in Illinois! To add insult to injury, it wasn't a "good" dirt road but loose dirt and gravel with a few hills to boot. The hardest thing was not knowing how long I'd be on it! At one point I shouted "FUCK!!!" at the top of my lungs to no one in particular. It was pointless, but it made me feel better. It only lasted about 3-4 miles, but it felt like much more than that. I eventually got back on a real road and rode into Blandford, Ma.

Blandford is a cute, small town, I'd never been there. Thankfully, there was a little general store on the side of the road. I stopped for a few minutes to rest and refuel. I'd been group texting good friends at home along the way complaining about the day in rather bold language. They were so supportive in their replies. That helped keep me going. They knew what my conditions were since they had the same 100 miles down the road in Providence.

The general store was great. Truly an old New England country store complete with wide wooden floorboards and a couple of rocking chairs in the corner. Two teenage boys were operating the counter and invited me to sit. I hesitated as my clothes were sweat-soaked, but they said: "Go ahead, sit, don't worry about it." Man did it feel good to sit down in the air conditioning. I drank two Cokes and had a few Kind bars as the steak and cheese had worn off long ago. As I sat there, I could see a puppy was sleeping beneath their feet under the register. It was so cute, only about 10 weeks old. It awoke, got up, and, after stretching, came over to say hi. That whole experience gave me another huge boost, and I was ready to tackle the last 20 miles of my day. It was already after 4:00 p.m. and I had been on the road for at least 8 hours.

There was a huge, long downhill leading me out of Blandford. It was great, and I felt like I deserved it by that point! I got into Westfield, 10 miles later, and was losing it. It was still ungodly hot; I was exhausted and getting "hangry." I opened a bottle of water as I rode down Main St. past Westfield State University. The road surface was terrible, I kept getting bounced around, and the water splashed all over getting my phone wet. I pulled over to dry

212

it off and spiked the water bottle to the ground. I was fed up and ready to be done at that point but had another 10 miles to get to my hotel in Springfield.

I got going again with my mantra running through my head. "Just keep going, just keep going...." as I watched the 10ths of miles tick down on my phone. I crossed the Connecticut River into Springfield. Hallelujah only a mile to go! I dragged myself into the hotel and checked in. As I was waiting for the person in front of me to finish, I glanced to my left and saw the greatest sight ever – there was a restaurant/bar right in the lobby! I wouldn't have to go any further that night! It was 6:30 p.m. over 10 hours since I'd started the day. It was the worst day of the entire journey, almost like someone was testing me saying "not so fast young lady, you have a way to go yet!"

I settled into my room and took my last shower of the journey, washing away all the sweat and toil before heading down to get dinner. As I sat at the bar eating dinner and having a drink the magnanimity of the whole trip sunk in. I couldn't believe I was watching the Red Sox on regular TV at the bar and not having to stream the game on my computer, or that I would be home and in my own bed tomorrow night. That I would finish. It was mind-blowing. I didn't know what to feel, happy, sad, exhausted, exuberant??? I was just numb.

After getting a good night's sleep, I got up early as the day would be another hot one and I wanted to start before 7:00. I told the Boys and Girls Club people I would be there by 2:30 – 3:00 p.m. I had 75 miles to ride and I didn't want to be late! As I rode the elevator down to the lobby, a man got on after me. He looked at me and the bike and said: "It's going to be pretty hot for that today."

"I know," I replied, "but I've been on the road for 2 months, and tonight I'll be home. Nothing's going to stop me today."

He chuckled and wished me luck as we headed out of the elevator to breakfast.

I ate and got going around 6:30 a.m. It wasn't too warm yet, and the streets of the city were quiet as I wound my way back to Rte. 20 for the last leg. I didn't need to rely on the maps the whole way that day. I just needed to get to Rte. 44 in western Rhode Island and follow it across the state to Providence. The closer I got, the more excited I was. I passed through the northeastern corner of Connecticut as I dipped down toward Rhode Island. I stopped and took a picture of the "Welcome to Connecticut" sign and texted it to my friends. "Yay!!" were the replies "you're almost here." I couldn't believe I would see them in a few short hours. I had padded in some extra time and knew I would stop at a Dunkin Donuts on Rte. 44 in Gloucester, RI to get something to eat and get ready for the final 15 miles to home!

Homecoming!

August 29, 2018

Well, I'm on my last pit-stop of this adventure, as I write this, I'm a little over 15 miles outside Providence in Chepachet, RI. Getting a last snack and cooling off before the homestretch. Figured it would be a good time to assess how I'm feeling about this day. That's a good question seeing the last two days have been brutal. I rode from Herkimer, NY to Clifton Park, NY on Monday, 80 miles. It may have been the easiest ride of the tour, flat and fast, did it in about 5.5 hours, like I said fast! Yesterday the road would not let me get off so easy!

Started from Albany at about 8:15 a.m. and headed for Springfield, Ma., 90 miles. I was determined to stay on schedule even though the weather called for an ultra hot and humid day. For once the weathermen were right - think it was 94. I also had to deal with the Berkshires - yay – mountains. How I had missed them over the last few weeks! The Berkshires are nothing like the Rockies or the Cascades, but hills are hills! It was a long day - this trip was just not going to let me go easily. Finally rolled into the hotel in Springfield at 6:30 p.m.

over 10 hours after I started. Totally beat and beat up but mission accomplished! Last night in a hotel for a while!

This morning dawned hot and humid again - expected to be hotter than yesterday - and it is! Seventy-six miles and I'll be home sweet home! I'm about sixty-two in so getting it done. The road threw in a few more hills just for kicks - but it's all downhill from where I sit now! To add insult to injury, I crossed into RI on a side road, so not even a sign to welcome me to the Ocean State! At least Google celebrated with me!

What am I feeling right now as this grand odyssey draws to a close? Hard to wrap my head around it but in a few words: relieved, happy, fulfilled, grateful, awestruck, in a state of disbelief. This has been an unforgettable journey. So many to thank - I will save that for a later date - but if you're reading this - "thank you." It's going to take some time to decompress and reflect on everything I've seen and done. People have asked me what my favorite part of the journey has been, and it's been hard to answer as every day when I finish, I just look forward to the next. I suspect, however, the answer lies 15 miles ahead of me in Providence at the corner of Ives and Wickenden Streets.

Those last 15 miles were surreal. I'd ridden the route before, so it was familiar, and it was home! I went through Harmony and noticed the street sign for the road where my grandparents had lived. Then I crossed Waterman Lake into Smithfield, then on into North Providence and Providence. I stopped beside the road next to LaSalle Academy and texted ahead to Nicole, I would be pulling up to the club in about 20 minutes. I went a little farther and stopped to snap a photo of the iconic Rhode Island State House on Smith Hill. I got down into the heart of the city, past the state house and then right onto Canal St. along the Providence River then past the courthouse where I'd spent so many hours of my working life. Then it was on to India Point and across the pedestrian bridge over Interstate 195 and onto Wickenden St. As I came up over the hill, I saw the people gathered at the corner of Ives St. at the Boys and Girls Club. I coasted around the corner as all the kids cheered and waved pom poms. My friends and family were there too. What a moment! I had done it! The smile couldn't be wiped from my face! The kids crowded around me while I still sat on the bike. They were all smiles and questions – it was the BEST!

AFTERMATH

After spending more than a year singularly focused on a specific task how does one adjust when that task is complete? The only experience I can compare it to is finishing a trial in court. You may have a huge caseload as a prosecutor or a public defender, perhaps 50 to 100 at any given moment, but when one is reached for trial, the others fade into oblivion. In the days leading to the trial, you are preparing your motions, your witnesses, your arguments to the exclusion of all else. The trial begins, and you must be acutely focused on every word said to determine if you should object. You craft your questions and your arguments to emphasize the evidence. Once the case goes to the jury, there is a reduction, but the tension of the unknown will be with you until the clerk calls your office, "We have a verdict." You rush to the courtroom the anticipation is palpable as the jury files into the room. Are they making eye contact with you? Are they staring at the floor? The verdict is pronounced and there is a rush of adrenaline or total deflation if it goes against your case. Either way, it's over, and the energy fades away. You walk back to your office, to all the files you've neglected during the trial feeling empty, but you start all over again.

That's how it felt to be finished with the ride. When all the festivities at the Boys and Girls Club were over that hot August afternoon, I loaded Crazy Horse into my sister's SUV and headed home. There was one more short celebration, my reunion with my dog Thatch. She was so happy to see me, that unconditional love that can only be felt between dog and owner. I was equally thrilled to see her and felt terrible about leaving her for two months. She's a rescue and had been abused in the few years before she came to me. I had her for about two and a half years when I started on the trip. She had come a long way in that time but was still very skittish. The reports while away weren't great. She was pissed off at me for abandoning her. But I had returned, and she was thrilled. She jumped on the couch and rolled over on her back. "Just please rub my belly," she said.

My sister left and there I was home, just me and the dog and cat. Everything was how I'd left it two months before. I slid back into normalcy, showered and dressed. Thatch and I headed out to Beth and Mike's for dinner. We went out the back door and Thatch jumped in the back of my car just as she had thousands of times before. It was all so routine, yet it was all so different. I was changed. I didn't quite know how yet, it would take weeks and months to figure out, though I'm not sure if even five months removed I know.

The weekend was a blur, it was Labor Day, so I had a few days to chill out and relax before starting back to work. My body still thought I was burning thousands of calories a day and I got hungry quickly even without exercising. I had lost 15-20 lbs. while eating more than I ever had in my life. So far, I've only put ten back on, hoping to keep it steady there. I went out for a 25-mile ride a few days after getting back. That was weird. I took out my road bike which felt like a feather after being on a loaded Crazy Horse every day for two months. I made my usual loop just to compare my fitness to pre-trip. My legs felt normal as if I'd just had my usual summer of riding. It was my lung capacity which surprised me. There's a short hill on the loop which I use to gauge my fitness through the season. Early on it generally leaves me sucking wind. Gradually throughout the summer, it gets easier. That day I almost didn't notice I had gone up it. I was lost in thought and didn't think about it until it was almost over. I guess I was in shape!

After the long weekend, I got back to work. I would need to rebuild my practice as I had wrapped up a lot of things before I left. It didn't take too long to get busy again, but I was having a difficult time concentrating. I felt adrift and unable to focus on any one task for long. It took a good six weeks to shake the feeling. There was a massive hole in my life. I no longer had one big thing to focus on, everything else seemed so inconsequential. For the previous fourteen months, I had predominantly focused on the ride, and it was the only focus while I was doing it. Now there was nothing. Sure, I had work and friends and my regular life back, but something was missing. I was even having a hard time writing this book, it seemed so anticlimactic.

The ride was still top of mind. I couldn't get through a day without running into someone who wanted to talk about it. That's still true even six months later. I received a lot of press coverage, which helped. The Providence Journal had run two front-page stories and covered my return home in a third piece. I was shocked when a local magazine "Rhode Island Monthly" wanted to include me as one of their people of the year. They did a nice write-up and put in a great picture with me and some kids from the Boys & Girls Clubs. Strangers would stop to speak with me, marveling at the feat. That was weird because having done it, it didn't feel so unusual.

One thing surprised me both during and after the journey was the reaction people were having. I had no idea going into it how much it would resonate with people. They opened their hearts and their wallets with contributions to the Club. I was stunned when we reached $75,000 in donations. The vast majority of those were small contributions, though we did have some corporate donors. The most shocking of all was an unsolicited $10,000 donation from a woman in the community. She had read about my journey, and it hit home with her. She had grown up in the Pacific Northwest and knew how important it was to learn how to swim. It was wonderful and humbling at the same time. People told me how reading my blogs had brought them to tears. Wow, I had no idea that my small contribution would affect people so much. I suppose it goes to show we all have the power to move mountains or just ride our bikes up them!

REFLECTIONS

About two months after I finished the journey, I was having coffee with a friend and catching up. He had run the Comrades Ultra Marathon several years before. It's a brutal 55-mile race in South Africa. It was interesting to talk to someone who had also completed a grueling physical challenge. He spoke about how hard the training runs were. He would routinely run from Woonsocket, RI to Newport, RI a 50-mile trek. It was not only grueling but solitary, much like my days alone on the bike. He asked me if I had discovered a mantra during my trip. He explained while he was in the middle of the race his mantra came to him "I was born here." I could much relate to that. You get to a certain point on these journeys where you become the journey, it is not only what you are doing but who you are. It is what you are "born" to be. I'm sure he thought long and hard about it while he was doing it and continues to do so.

During the journey, I too had discovered a mantra, though I hadn't thought about it in those terms until he asked me the question. My one resonating thought every day, particularly during hard stretches, was "just keep going." It was that simple. Just keep going. It began on that third day as I climbed McKenzie Pass. It was hot and steep; at times I could only pedal a few hundred yards before my

225

legs turned into jelly and I was in danger of falling over. I simply kept telling myself to "just keep going." I broke down the journey by the mile markers on the side of the road, "just keep going to the next mile marker," then you can stop and have some water. "You must be halfway to the next marker you can stop and take a drink then, just keep going." The mantra was most prevalent in the mountains. I was pedaling or pushing Crazy Horse up those steep faces, and 65 miles would be broken down to miles, then half miles, then yards between stops. It was the only way to do it. I couldn't think about the whole 65 miles; I would have been so overwhelmed I would probably still be sitting on the side of the road crying at the enormity of it all. The only way I would do it was to break it into manageable pieces and celebrate each one as a victory even if it was only 500 yards. Just keep going.

That didn't stop when I got past the Cascades or the Rockies but continued into the Plains. How could I possibly do 95 to 100 miles per day for three or four days in a row without telling myself to "just keep going?" When I was heading into St. Paul after riding 100 miles with still 15 miles to go? "Just keep going." When I was routed onto an awful dirt and gravel road 80 miles into a 90-mile day in 93-degree heat just outside of Springfield, there was no choice. "Just keep going." It is what kept me going every day for two months. I couldn't stop to think about what I was doing. It just had to be done, day after day, mile after mile.

As I reflect on the journey and how it fits into the rest of my life it becomes clear "just keep going" is not merely the mantra of my journey, it is the mantra of my life. I have suffered severe depression for most of my life, though it wasn't until I was into my 30's that I identified it and not until almost 50 that I conquered it. In looking back, it's clear I survived because I just kept going.

Depression is a horrible disease. It's not like having the flu or breaking a bone it's invisible, so much so, a person may not even be aware they have it for years. That's what happened to me. I would go through inexplicably low periods. I couldn't understand why I felt so bad. I lived a successful life. I had excellent grades all the way through law school, been a great athlete, done well at any job I tried, been in the best of health. Why did I feel like a failure? Why did I want to sit in my house alone reading books and drinking until I fell asleep? Everyone believed I was successful, just not me.

When I was 35, with the help of a friend, I sought help. Unfortunately, I didn't trust it. It was 2001, and mental health was just coming into focus as a true health condition and wasn't "just all in one's head." I had grown up in a family of amazing health, the most serious thing was a bad cold for the most part. My grandmother had lived to ninety-eight without taking more than an aspirin, and my

227

mother was on the same track. When the psychiatrist told me I was "sick," I couldn't comprehend it. I was fine, just look at me, I can run marathons! "No," she said, "your brain is sick. You need medication." I resisted.

Davis's don't do medication.

"Prove to me that my brain is sick." I declared.

"Well," the doctor responded, "we can open your skull, take a slice of the brain and analyze it if you want proof."

"Fine! I'll try the stupid medication."

It seemed to work some, but I still didn't feel great. I kept going with life, working, playing, socializing, but I always felt like a failure. On the outside, I appeared to be my usual self, but those inner demons still lurked. I went through the next ten years like this.

Finally, I felt good and opened my law practice, how hard could that be?! Everyone told me I'd be great. I was smart, and I knew a lot of people, it will be easy. At the same time, I was getting irritated by the side effects of the meds. I had severe night sweats and couldn't seem to shake the few extra pounds I wanted to lose. I stopped taking them, not bright on my part. Having gone off and on a few times in the past, I knew it wasn't easy. I knew there would be withdrawals, but I had no idea it would be as bad as it was. No one explained each time you go off these drugs the withdrawal effect is worse than the time before.

I plunged into the darkest hole I had ever experienced. I would wake up in the predawn hours and not be able to get back to sleep. The only thought in my mind was wishing I was dead. I was never suicidal. I am neither brave nor cowardly enough. I just didn't want to be alive. I would force myself to go into my office but would get there and be paralyzed with fear and anxiety. I had to get clients, I had to learn everything about the law I didn't know. I would sit there tying myself into knots.

Again, I sought help. My original therapist had passed away several years earlier, and my general practitioner was prescribing my medications. I hadn't consulted her when I stopped taking them. Not the brightest idea. I was referred to a new doctor and saw her within a few days. At the initial appointment, we went through the usual rigamarole of "tell me a little about yourself." As I was going through my life's achievements and my history with her, she sat back and stared at me. "You're really smart and accomplished," she said.

"Yes, I suppose you could say that," I replied.

Her next words rocked me like an earthquake. "Stop trying to figure this out and cure yourself. Just accept that your brain is sick."

She elaborated that I was trying to figure out why there was something wrong with me and cure it by myself. She explained this was impossible. I needed to allow myself to be sick and to heal, just as if I had a broken leg or the flu.

If all I wanted to do was lie on the couch and watch "Law & Order" reruns so be it. She gave me permission to be sick. Stop pressuring yourself to will your way out of this. Stop going to the office trying to work your way through it. Give yourself space and time to recover. A new medication was also part of the plan. I did what she prescribed and haven't looked back once.

I just kept going.

It took nearly 50 years to know myself and come to grips with this terrible disease. The bike journey represents a true turning point in my life. As I explained, in the spring of 2017 I was restless and needed something to focus on.

Was this going to be the onset of another bout of depression? No, it was the exact opposite. Instead of going down into that dark hole again I kept going right on past it and set my sights on this journey. I wanted to be alive, not dead.

If the journey was what I needed to do so be it. Perhaps it's what I needed to do to indeed be over it. Or, maybe it has nothing at all to do with my depression. Either way, I know I'm a better person having done it.

Every day I am asked if I would do the ride again. Every time I'm asked, I shrug and say, "I don't know." I do know there will be other journeys and I can't wait to find out what they are.

Meanwhile, I will just keep going.

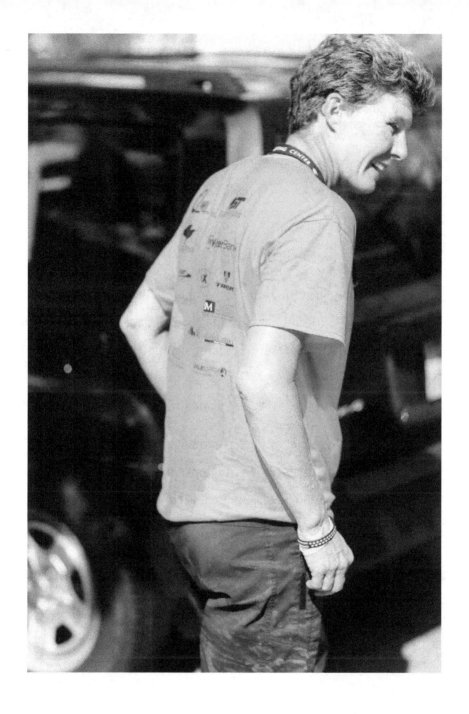

ABOUT THE AUTHOR

Judy Davis has accomplished much in her life. She has been an athlete, a police officer, taken on the challenge of law school while working full-time, served as both a Prosecutor with the Rhode Island of Department of Attorney General and as a private defense attorney with her own law firm.

Taking on the challenge of a cross-country bike ride is another of these many challenges.

Seeing the need for supporting the important swimming program at the Fox Point Boys and Girls Club, she combined her trip with a most successful fund-raising campaign, raising over $70,000 to date. The money will support the life-saving swimming program for young boys and girls at the club.

By opening up about her personal and, up to this point, private but successful struggle with depression, she sends a message of hope to those who live with this debilitating condition.

Contact the author through JEBWizard Publishing (JEBWizardPublishing@Gmail.com)

CPSIA information can be obtained
at www.ICGtesting.com
Printed in the USA
LVHW060204190619
621681LV00007B/13/P